PUBLIC ADMINISTRATION IN PALESTINE PAST AND PRESENT

Usamah Shahwan

University Press of America,® Inc.
Lanham · Boulder · New York · Toronto · Oxford

Copyright © 2003 by
University Press of America,® Inc.
4501 Forbes Boulevard
Suite 200
Lanham, Maryland 20706
UPA Acquisitions Department (301) 459-3366

PO Box 317
Oxford
OX2 9RU, UK

All rights reserved
Printed in the United States of America
British Library Cataloging in Publication Information Available

Library of Congress Control Number: 2003110066
ISBN 0-7618-2688-2 (paperback : alk. ppr.)

♾™ The paper used in this publication meets the minimum
requirements of American National Standard for Information
Sciences—Permanence of Paper for Printed Library Materials,
ANSI Z39.48—1984

*To my wife Nabilah
and my two children Nael and Tarik*

❧❦

The worst forms of tyranny are those so subtle, so deeply ingrained, so thoroughly controlling as not ever to be consciously experienced.

— Michael Parenti,
Democracy For The Few

CONTENTS

PREFACE xi

INTRODUCTION xiii

CHAPTER 1: THE OTTOMAN
RULE IN PALESTINE (1517-1917) 1

Administrative Divisions 1

Executive, Legislative and Judicial Administration 3

Local Government and Ottoman Administrative
Policies Toward the Local Population 7

CHAPTER 2: PALESTINE UNDER
THE BRITISH MANDATE (1920- 1948) 13

The Military Government and Civil Administration 13

Executive, Legislative and Judicial Administration 16

Local Government and the British Administrative
Policies Towards the Local Population 19

CHAPTER 3: JORDANIAN ADMINISTRATION
IN THE WEST BANK (1950-1967) 23

The Process of Integrating the West Bank
into the Hashemite Kingdom of Jordan 23

Executive, Legislative and Judicial Administration 26

Local Government: Municipalities and Village Councils 31

Jordanian Administrative Policies in the West Bank 35

CHAPTER 4: EGYPTIAN ADMINISTRATION
IN THE GAZA STRIP (1948-1967) 39

The Egyptian Military Government in the Gaza Strip ... 39

Local Government and the Refugee Problem 41

CHAPTER 5: THE WEST BANK AND GAZA
UNDER ISRAELI MILITARY OCCUPATION (1967-1994) ... 45

Structural Changes and the
Annexation of East Jerusalem 45

The Military Orders and Their Impact
on Public Administration 49

Local Government and Grass-Root Organizations 51

Municipal and Village Councils 51

Grass-Root Organizations:
Objectives and Impact 53

An Assessment of Public Administration
in Palestine under Israeli Occupation 54

The Civil Administration 54

Municipal and Village Councils 55

Lack of Judicial Review 57

CHAPTER 6: PUBLIC ADMINISTRATION UNDER
THE PALESTINIAN NATIONAL AUTHORITY 61

The Legal Framework: The Oslo Accords of 1993 64

The Legislative Council 65
The Executive Authority 67
The Civil Service 68
Human Resource Management 72
Fiscal Management 74
Local Government 76
Financing Local Councils 78
The Judiciary 79
The Socio-Cultural Context of
    Palestinian Public Administration 81

CHAPTER 7: ISSUES IN PALESTINIAN
PUBLIC ADMINISTRATION AND THE
THORNY ROAD TOWARD REFORM 87
    Political Appointees 87
    Women in Leadership Positions 89
    Limited Sovereignty 91
    The Role of Non-Government Organizations 92
    The Thorny Road Toward Reform 94

CHAPTER 8: CONCLUSIONS 101

NOTES 119

INDEX 117

ABOUT THE AUTHOR 123

PREFACE

The decision to write this book was prompted by a paucity of research dealing with the development of government institutions in this sensitive region of the world. Public administration has been a neglected area and its impact on public policies in the Middle East has not received the attention it deserves. To put political and economic developments in modern Palestine in proper perspective, it is necessary to trace the historical development of government bureaucracies during the last two centuries. In this part of the world, history exerts tremendous influence on the present.

A significant portion of the dilemmas and controversies plaguing public policies in Palestine at present cannot be understood without digging up their distant roots in earlier epochs. The recurrence of the same phenomena is dazzling.

The study presents an overview of the development of public administration in Palestine since the second quarter of the nineteenth century and up to the present. It is targeted at both the common reader and the scholar interested in the field.

The work is a compilation of various studies carried out by the author between 1992-2002, some of which was sponsored by international and local organizations. The methodology is based on data collected from books, published and unpublished documents, official statistics, newspaper reports and the background experience of the author. The experience drawn through my involvement for ten years in a number of seminars and training courses sponsored by different Palestinian and international organizations and directed at Palestinian government employees from different ministries was an eye opener that revealed a host of problems and unresolved issues. The sources consulted throughout the research represent a multiplicity of viewpoints and orientations. Strenuous efforts have been exerted in order to come up with an objective assessment taking into consideration the complexities and the sensitivities of the issues tackled.

I was writing the last chapter of the book when the September 2000 uprising erupted creating new facts on the ground. So I found it necessary to go back and make certain adjustments in view of the new developments that brought into sharp focus, more than ever before, the serious shortcomings and leakages in the Palestinian government bureaucracy. Ironically, the long hours and days of military curfews provided me with ample opportunity to write, as I was freed from routine daily life obligations and nuisances, though not oblivious to the misery around and the sufferings of the innocent victims from both sides of the divide.

My efforts to write the book would not have produced the desired fruits had it not been for the support and encouragement of the Faculty of Management at Bethlehem University and in particular, Fadi Kattan, Dean of the school who, in spite of the financial difficulties facing the University was able to procure funds from the Faculty's budget to provide assistance. I also want to express my gratitude for the Secretary of the Faculty and a former student of mine, Mary Zeit for her invaluable help in typing and formatting parts the draft. I would also like to extend my thanks to Br. Joseph Lowenstein, Dr. Hanna Tushyeh and Stephen Henry from the English Department for their assistance in proof-reading and editing the manuscript. I could not forget my students who constantly provided insight and inspiration throughout the period the book was being prepared. The responsibility for the contents of this book, of course, rests with me.

Usamah Shahwan,
Bethlehem, Palestine

INTRODUCTION

The West Bank and Gaza, which represent approximately 22 percent of historic Palestine has captured the world's attention during the past two years. The tragic events, resulting from the violent confrontations between the Israeli army and the Palestinians, have cast a dark shadow over the prospects of public sector development in Palestine. Already fragile and struggling to survive in light of the precarious economic and political conditions in the area, the public administration system that evolved in the aftermath of the Oslo Accords of 1993 sustained a crippling blow as a consequence. The successive military incursions that started in the months of March and April 2002, and continued unabated throughout the summer caused massive destruction to both the civil infrastructure and public institutions in addition to the economic havoc it wreaked on the Palestinian community. The fledgling government service was the largest employer in the country with jobs totaling around 130,000 employees in both the civil and security apparatus. The devastation of many public institutions has inevitably impacted the functioning and performance of other vital services like telecommunication, electricity, water and banking which depended on the Palestinian Authority for regulation and security. Rehabilitation of the battered infrastructure will require more than repairing the physical damage. There is a strong need for a serious and objective review of the policies that had existed prior to the Israeli incursions particularly in the areas of planning, financial accountability and human resources. There has been an enormous pressure from both the Palestinian public and the international community for drastic political and administrative changes in the PNA in order to provide for accountability and transparency in the conduct of public affairs.

The territories of the West Bank and Gaza, including East Jerusalem, are home to approximately 3 million people of whom more than 400,000 are registered refugees living in 29 refugee camps. The area is 6000 square kilometers (2316 sq. miles). Palestine changed hands five times during the past century. The region under discussion was ruled by the Turkish Ottoman Empire, England, Jordan (West Bank) and Egypt (Gaza), and Israel before the Palestinian National Authority took control of the two regions following the Oslo Accords in 1994. The population are 98% Arab Palestinians and there are about 230,000 Jewish settlers living in 150 settlements. The West Bank and Gaza have one of the highest fertility rates in the world (3.4- 3.8), and around 50% of the population is under 16 years of age. Economically, Palestine is not well developed. Before the current uprising, GDP reached approximately 3 billion dollars with a relatively low per capita income ranging between 1800-2500 dollars in the West Bank and 1000-1500 dollars in the Gaza Strip. Services constituted the largest portion of the GDP (50%) followed by agriculture (28%), small industry (8%) and construction (15%).

The study spans five historic epochs: the Ottoman, British, Jordanian, Israeli and Palestinian. It would be difficult to comprehend the special features of public administration in Palestine without linking them to the historical development of the art of governance in this part of the world during the last two centuries. A number of "idiosyncrasies" that characterize the structure and function of government bureaucracies in the Middle East have their roots in the not-too distant past.

Despite conspicuous differences among the various regimes that dominated Palestine, the attitude and behavior of the political rulers towards the local population exhibited identical orientations and tendencies. *Public administration at both the central and local levels was used as a means of political and economic control.* The policies implemented were designed to strengthen the hegemony of the occupying power over the populace. A by-product of such policies was the subservient status of the local administration vis-à-vis the central authority that continues to be a major feature of government in Palestine up to the present. The ideology of administration in this part of the world has been an ideology of domination rather than of development. This conclusion represents the most important finding of this research. This has inadvertently led to the emergence of a distinctive feature not very common in other developing countries, and that is the important and unprecedented role of non-government organizations in the life of the Palestinian community. The vital role of these organizations has been clearly demonstrated during the first *Intifadah* (uprising) 1987-1992 and later during the second *Al-Aqsa* uprising in September 2000 when the whole edifice of public bureaucracy collapsed and essential public services were paralyzed.

Part of the reasons, which rendered government administration inefficient and ineffective during the periods spanned, was the poor choice of personnel especially at leadership levels and the lack of credible human resource strategies. Public employment has been used as a political tool and in many instances the public sector became a choice of last resort for unskilled manpower looking for jobs. This has had a tremendous negative effect on the chances for economic and social development. Attempts at administrative reform have been largely unsuccessful and were often cosmetic focusing on non-essential technical and clerical aspects of the public office. Widespread corruption has become a recurring feature of government service and has often caused a serious drain on the limited financial resources of the country. One should bear in mind, however, that we are not talking about a "traditional" public administration in the sense of an executive apparatus in an independent and sovereign state but rather an administrative body that has evolved over time to serve the particular interests of whoever was in control. It has never been designed to deliver public services to a clientele who democratically elected their government. The uppermost priority of such a body was to provide a mechanism of control for the political elite over the local population. This has tremendously slowed the pace of development in the Palestinian Territories especially when one takes into account the fact that the private sector has always been economically and financially weak with limited resources for any significant projects of its own. Therefore, it would be unrealistic to talk about socio-economic growth in Palestine in the absence of a supportive and qualified government bureaucracy that is ready and willing to forge a strong partnership with the private sector. The opportunities or probably the threats generated by the phenomenon of globalization makes it imperative for any future Palestinian authority to start a process of revitalization in the government executive branch aimed at modernizing the system to cope with the ever increasing challenges of globalization.

Recently the Palestinian National Authority has been under attack for its alleged failure to stop public officials from exploiting the public service for personal gain and parochial purposes that have lead to unbridled corruption and malfeasance in many spheres. It is true that the phenomenon of government corruption is rampant in many developing countries but the evolving Palestinian government system can ill-afford such unlawful practices at a time when it is almost totally dependent on foreign financial support from donor countries. It is extremely important at this stage to setup an adequate system of financial control and audit that ensures accountability and transparency. This can only be done through a continuous process of democratization and empowerment of institutions that are the core of civil society. A viable civil service is an illusion without an independent judiciary that acts as a safety valve against possible abuse of government power besides providing a legal interpretation of public policies. The judiciary is an integral part of any government system in a democracy. In recent times it has begun to play a significant role in setting national policies in various democratic countries. The Supreme Court of the United States of America, through a number of landmark rulings especially with regard to civil rights, has been able to introduce revolutionary changes in the life of the American public. However, the focus of this study will be primarily, but not exclusively, on the executive and legislative branches of public administration in Palestine. Reference to judicial issues will be made when these issues impact the structure and performance of certain government agencies as should be expected under such circumstances.

In the last few months, and as a result of the mounting pressures on the PNA, a number of steps have been taken to reform the government system. The executive branch was reshuffled, changes were made in the security apparatus for the purpose of integrating it into a more manageable body, and fiscal measures were initiated to provide for more transparency and accountability. How adequate these steps are and whether the measures taken will lead to public sector improvement and efficiency depend primarily on the political developments on the ground. There are few places in the world where politics and administration are so interlocked as in the case of Palestine.

1

THE OTTOMAN RULE IN PALESTINE (1517-1917)

The expanding Ottoman Empire crowned its campaign of conquests in 1516 by conquering the countries of the Near East and expelling the corrupt and inept *Memluks*. The event marked a critical turning point in the history of the region as it heralded a new era that was destined to become one of the longest occupations in the history of mankind. With the exception of a brief interruption between the years 1831- 1840, the Ottoman Turks ruled Palestine from 1517 to 1917. Four centuries of Turkish domination brought many changes to life and society in the Middle East.

Administrative Divisions

Politically and administratively, Palestine was not accorded an independent status during the Ottoman reign. Throughout that period, Palestine was part of the "Greater Syria," which included present day Lebanon, Jordan and Syria proper.[1] For the purpose of administration, Syria was divided into three *wilayats* or administrative divisions, and each *wilayat* was sub-divided into *sanjaks (districts)*. Palestine was administratively part of the *wilayat* of

Damascus, which had ten *sanjaks* embracing Jerusalem and Nablus.[2] It continued to be under the authority of the *wilayat* of Damscus till 1840 when it was placed under the jurisdiction of the *wilayat* of Beirut.

Each *wilayat* was entrusted to a Turkish *wali* (governor) who was responsible directly to the government in the capital Constantinople. According to the "Law of the *Wilayats*" issued during the reign of Sultan Abdul-Aziz in 1864, each *wilayat* was subdivided into smaller units, called *sanjaks, kazas* and *nahiyats*.[3] Legislations issued in 1871 granted the *wali* extensive and far-reaching powers in security and civilian matters. His authority covered the areas of finance education, public works, police, civil and criminal affairs, law enforcement, appointment of provincial officials, supervision of tax collection, development of schools, and promotion of trade and agriculture. He was also granted special powers to use the regular army in addition to the police in certain circumstances to curb disturbances and deal with any challenges to public security.[4] Almost the same powers were granted to the governors under the British, Jordanian and Israeli regimes.

The earliest attempt to modernize administration in the regions ruled by the Ottoman Turks was carried out by a rebellious leader, Muhammad Ali Pasha of Egypt, who challenged Ottoman sovereignty and occupied Syria and Palestine between 1831-1840. In order to consolidate his Power, the new ruler introduced significant political, social and administrative reforms that paved the way for a more comprehensive reform movement called the "*tanzimat*" ten years later.

Around the middle of the nineteenth century, and probably due to the increasing influence of the West, especially France, a new administrative re-organization called *tanzimat* of the territories under the Ottoman's jurisdiction took place. These so-called reforms were copied from the French system, and the Ottoman Empire was divided into administrative units corresponding to their French counterparts.[5] The administrative picture that emerged after the *tanzimat* revealed that the administrative "reforms" had been motivated by expedient political considerations rather than by a desire to improve the welfare of the subjects of the empire. Nationalist aspirations, the economic development of the local populations, and the ethnic and cultural differences among the multitudes of races populating the empire did not constitute the primary motives for those who engineered the reforms. Writing in 1867, an Englishman expressed the following observations about the so-called reforms:

> Sultan Mahmud II tranquilized their fears, and justified their hopes, by his tanzimat (reforms) proclaimed four months after his accession. This famous proclamation, conceived in a spirit of clemency and tolerance, inaugurated a new era for Turkey. The direct power of death by decapitation was taken from scores of vizirs; the indirect power of death by vexation, from hundreds of inferior stations. Oriental ductility was severely tested. An ensanguined nation was ordered to be gentle, and the order was obeyed. Pashas, used to rule with the sabre were required to rule by exhortation. Mudirs and agas, wont to admonish rayas with the stick, were enjoined to be civil to them. The exhaustion of the nation, after twenty years of unparalleled suffering, favoured the experiment; anything for quiet was the universal aspiration. The Ottomans, with the instincts of a dominant race, adapted themselves to altered circumstances, they leant upon their prestige, and it did not fail them. Fatalists, they were not sorry to see their Sultan cease, of his own accord, to be the direct instrument of fate in regard to them.[6]

Executive, Legislative and Judicial Administration

The Ottoman Empire in the second half of the nineteenth century reflected a mosaic of political phenomena that were often in stark contradiction to each other. Formally, the constitution promulgated in 1876 by Sultan Abdul-Hamid II envisaged a political model of a modern state based on the democratic principles of the West. It formally provided for a strict observance of *shariat*- the Islamic religious law- and the upholding of the special privileges of the Sultan.[7] In practice the Sultan continued to function as the supreme executive authority without any significant limitations on his power. This was not only in contradiction to the principle of the separation of powers which the Ottoman government claimed to respect, but it also violated the Islamic principle of *shura* (consultation) to which the Sultan was bound as the caliph of all Moslems.

Constantinople was the capital of the Empire and the center of power. To help them carry out their policies, the sultans were assisted by administrative machinery composed of the various ministries and officers of the court. In this respect, special attention should be paid to the vital role played by the army in the political affairs of the state and in helping to strengthen the grip of the autocratic rulers. Together with the reorganization of the administration that took place around the middle of the nineteenth century, a comprehensive reform of the Ottoman army was carried out. General conscription was imposed and in a few years a professional force composed entirely of Moslem conscripts and numbering over 150,000 regulars backed by reservists emerged.[8] Such a formidable force, by that time's standards was destined to take an active part in the administration of the Empire as well as in the battlefield. The army's interference in politics reached a climax during the period between 1909-1918 when an extremist nationalistic movement called the "Young Turks" that was composed entirely of young military cadets staged a coup-de-tat and deposed Sultan Abdul-Hamid II. The Junta established a military dictatorship.[9] They started to take extreme political and administrative measures that antagonized the Arab and other ethnic minorities in the Empire leading to insurgencies in many localities and in turn to cruel reprisals by the Turkish authorities. The unmitigated influence of the Ottoman army in the affairs of the state following the Coup continued unabated till 1918 when the Empire was defeated in the First World War.

In discussing the legislative powers of the Ottoman governments in the nineteenth and the early twentieth century, the Western conceptions of "separation of powers" and "checks and balances" were irrelevant. It was evident that despite the movements for administrative and political reforms in the middle of the nineteenth century, the sultans continued to have absolute powers till 1909. Although Abdul-Hamid II promised to uphold the new liberal Constitution of 1876 it was suspended shortly after he assumed power and remained so for thirty years.[10] It should be noted, however, that conservative Moslem leaders played a negative role in this regard. It seemed as if there was a tacit agreement between the sultans and the Council of *Ulamas* (religious leaders) to perpetuate the status-quo in which both parties benefited. On the one hand, the sultan would slow down the process of modernization, on the other hand, the conservative clergy would withhold any criticism of the sultan's monopoly of political power and unlimited privileges. The *shariat* or Islamic law derived from the Koran remained the source of all legislation and any deviation from this tradition faced a stiff resistance from the Religious High Council whose members regarded themselves as the guardians of Islam. However, the *tanzimat* started in 1839 during the reign of Sultan Mahmud II, formally introduced a number of progressive reforms in the legislative branch of the political structure by guaranteeing certain basic rights such as the security of life and property, the elimination of arbitrary methods of assessing and collecting taxes and equality for all citizens under the law.[11] In practice these reforms never materialized. Sultan Mahmud II sought advice from a number of councils whose members he himself appointed. The most important of these councils was the Council of Justice, which played a key role during the *tanzimat* period and was given quasi-legislative powers[12] But the fact that the members of such councils were chosen by the sultan, and were not elected freely from the populace indicated that they were mere instruments used to give an impression of legitimacy to his political powers rather than being representative bodies of the public. It was, to use a modern term "co-optation." The Palestinians during the period under discussion had no elected bodies representing them before the central government of Constantinople. The *wali* and the few notables from the area appointed by the sultan in his councils of deliberation served only their own interests and those of the government. It is no wonder that the economic and social conditions of Palestine under the Ottoman rule were appalling and the people were seldom able to communicate their needs and aspirations to the ruling circles in the state.

The process of modernization, embodied by the *tanzimat* in the middle of the nineteenth century, was expanded to include the judicial system in the empire. The principal motive behind the reorganization of the legal system seemed to be the gradual opening of the Empire to the outside world, especially the European powers, and the commercial ties which such openness entailed. As early as 1841, Rashid Pasha authorized the establishment of the commercial court to settle commercial disputes between natives and foreigners, based on a new code adopted from the French system.[13] Other important measures followed almost immediately. Between 1840 and 1858 the Ottoman penal law and land law were both codified marking a turning point in the movement to adopt, for the first time in the history of the empire, a secular law besides the religious law "shariat" which predominated till then.[14] The process of judicial modernization, however, was met with relentless resistance by the Moslem religious establishment that felt threatened by what they perceived as a secular trend posing risks to its hegemony over the private affairs of individuals.

The new Court of Justice established by Rashid pasha was suspended by the Sultan following the opposition of the Religious High Council who viewed the step as a deviation from Islamic principles.[15] Probably due to Western pressure, the program of judicial secularization continued, however, the religious courts were not abolished; but their jurisdiction was confined to personal and family relationships. The system of civil courts was developed further in 1879-880, adopting the French procedural codes especially with regard to the admission of evidence.[16] Ten years earlier a high court of appeal and cassation was established as well as a *conseil d'état* responsible for drafting administrative regulations.[17] In Palestine, civil courts and religious courts operated side by side. The new administrative measures failed to produce significant improvement in the plight of the local citizens. Local people could not resort to the judicial system to redress any wrongdoing committed by government officials or to protest the harsh measures often applied by government representatives against the peasantry and in many cases against religious minorities. It is noteworthy that the *conseil d'état* was prohibited by the Sultan from offering any protection for the property and the person of the subject against the central government. The Council was in fact impotent in litigations involving the citizens versus the administration.[18] Furthermore, the courts had no authority in cases involving government employees and their superiors. During 1913 - 1917, the Young Turks who took over the Empire introduced what were described as innovative reforms in the judicial system, which included the three areas of land law, civil law and personal status, and the reforms were incorporated into the legal structure of Palestine.[19] However, the breakout of the First World War and the chaotic situation in the provinces resulting from military operations prevented their implementation. In general the judicial system in Palestine was an extension of the administrative system of government rather than an autonomous branch of the state with the power to ensure universal justice for all.

Local Government and Ottoman Administrative Policies Toward the Local Population

Palestine, with the rest of the Arab regions of the Ottoman Empire, was impacted by the administrative reforms in the last seventy years of Ottoman rule. The reforms, especially those that took place during 1840-1870, were inspired by the French model of administration. Formally, steps were taken to provide representation for local population in the provinces. The small administrative council called *majlis umumi* was set up in each *wilayat*. Its members were elected deputies representing the sub-districts and each *majlis* included Moslems and non-Moslems. Administrative councils met once a year for a period of forty days at the capital of the *wilayat*. In every *wilayat* and alongside the provincial assembly, there existed other administrative and judicial councils called *majalis idara,* which performed administrative and judicial functions. Their members were partly elected and partly appointed. In small administrative units, district councils under the name of *majlis-al-nahiyat* were created. Each council was headed by a *mudir* (director).

Jerusalem was the only town in Palestine that had a municipal council. The exact date of its creation has been a controversial matter, but the majority of sources believe it came into existence around 1857 by direct order from the Sultan. In 1877, the Ottoman Municipal laws were issued, according to which municipal councils were set up in cities and towns. In the last days of the Ottoman rule in Palestine there were 22 municipal councils, Eight in the West Bank and one in Gaza city. Council members were elected by direct vote every four years. Half of them were replaced every two years. Their number ranged between 6-12 individuals depending on the population size of the town. Only the chairman of the council received a salary from the government and all other members acted in an honorary capacity. The functions of the council included the supervision of buildings, streets, lighting, market control, etc. To be eligible for election to municipal councils, one had to be over thirty, and a payer of a property tax. The above law specified the sources of municipal revenue, which included licence fees, property tax, building and construction fees, fines etc.

In reality, the creation of the local councils did not democratize Ottoman administration or helped bring the government closer to the people. On the contrary the power of the Turkish rulers grew with the creation of these councils as the councils "provided the all powerful pasha with a fresh method for clothing his own will in a legitimate garb."[20] A critical analysis of the Ottoman Municipal laws of 1877 reveals that the real objective of the Ottoman rulers was to achieve tighter control of the local population and improve the efficiency of tax collection methods. The type of central-local relations that these laws embodied reflected a master-slave model rather than a system of equal partnership in the governance of the people. Articles 4 and 19 of the above laws are clear examples of this. According to article 4, the president of the local council was to be chosen by the government from among the elected council members who actually served only in an honorary capacity with half of them being replaced every two years. Article 19 stipulated that every elected council member should be able to speak Turkish to understand the orders issued by the Ottoman *wali* and other government officials. Taking into consideration the fact that illiteracy was almost universal in the Middle East during that period we might conclude that only a privileged few could be elected to local councils. The town councils were exclusively composed of the urban and rural land- lords, and other classes were practically unrepresented.[21]

Further, the concept of development, as an important role of local government councils was non-existent. Article 3 of the above law which referred to the duties and responsibilities of the town council included only those duties normally designed for maintenance of the town such as, lighting, general hygiene, collection of fees, safeguarding public property etc, and nothing was mentioned of the responsibility of the local council in social and economic development which is an essential function of local government.

A unique pattern of administration called "confessional decentralization" was maintained, whereby the non-Moslem religious groups (millets) were organized into communities. The religious leader of each community exercised administrative powers in matters relating to personal status but through confessional rather than territorial organs.[22]

However, there seems to be little historical evidence to indicate that the reforms and the establishment of local councils produced any significant change in the structure and functions of the Ottoman administration in Palestine. Even after the enactment of the new constitution of 1908, which envisaged more autonomy in self-government in non-Turkish provinces, things did not look much different. The Young Turks who came to power in 1908 and deposed Abdul-Hamid II proceeded to tighten their grip on the central bureaucracy, further alienating the inhabitants of non-Turkish provinces.[23]

Ottoman administration was highly centralized. It was a vast empire that sought to control a wide variety of peoples and cultures scattered over three continents. The two primary objectives of the administrative machinery that the Ottomans instituted in the conquered lands were maintaining control over the local populace and ensuring a continuous flow of tax revenues from the provinces to the treasury. The method of appointment to the position of the *wali* reflected the central government's tyrannical attitude and disregard for the common people. The public position was offered to the highest bidder, and in such instances the *wali* often exploited his position to accumulate wealth, and corruption was rampant in the provinces of the Empire as in the capital.[24]

The army (called the Janissary in the early period) exercised much influence in the affairs of the state, and this influence increased tremendously at the end of the nineteenth century when the military interfered in the administration of the country and provided the central government with public officials including *viziers* (cabinet ministers) and provincial governors.[25]

In analyzing the administrative structure and functions of the Ottoman administration in Palestine, in general, one could not ignore the socio-economic context within which the administration operated during that historical period. The areas were economically impoverished; the majority of the population was composed of peasants and craftsmen. For the former, agricultural land that constituted their only source of income was under the control of the Turkish pashas and their protégées. An agricultural tax called "tithe" was 10-12% of agricultural yield and tax collection was franchised to private individuals who were accompanied by government troops to enforce tax collection. These individuals levied more than the percentage determined by government to secure their cut, and many of them made a fortune out of the miseries of poor peasants. Those peasants who could not pay had their produce and property confiscated. Illiteracy was almost universal. The official language was Turkish, which only a few locals could write or speak. Administrative organization in that period was carried out without much regard for public interest or welfare but was obviously intended to serve the interests of the central government in the capital. This attitude seems to be so trenchant that all the rulers who assumed power after the Ottomans perpetuated it. The way that small area of the West Bank was administratively organized, reflected the Ottoman's approach that ignored the importance of both geography and demography in administrative division. For example, the *sanjak* (district) of Nablus embracing the city of Nablus and the adjacent towns of Jenin and Tulkarem and the surrounding area in the south including Jaffa, Hebron, Gaza and Beersheba was an Ottoman district responsible directly to Constantinople.[26] Other towns falling within the same geographic unit were administratively controlled by other capitals under Ottoman jurisdiction.

Like any other autocratic regime, the concept of good government, as servant of the people was alien to Turkish rulers. The subjects did not expect much from their rulers in terms of welfare and prosperity. A Turkish liberal writing in 1872 about the "Functions of the State" probably reflected the attitude of many people living under Ottoman rule:

> There must be no doubt that the government is neither the father nor the teacher, neither the guardian nor the tutor of the people. If it renders service to the education of the individual, the prosperity of the realm, the advancement of mankind, the progress of civilization, it will contribute significantly to the welfare of itself, of its people, and indeed all of the world... But even if it confines itself to its primary duty, which is the maintenance of justice, can you complain? Have we any right to require it to serve us as nursemaid.[27]

2

PALESTINE UNDER THE BRITISH MANDATE 1920-1948

The Military Government and Civil Administration

As the vanquished Turkish army started to retreat following its crushing defeat by the allies at the end of the First World War, the British forces were advancing and taking over positions vacated by the Turks in the Arab Near East. The occupation of Palestine by the British was completed in two stages. By the end of December 1917 the areas south of Jerusalem and Jaffa: Beersheba, Gaza, Ashkelon, Majdal, Ramleh, Ramallah, Jericho, Bethlehem and Hebron had been captured by the British forces and placed under military administration. It took almost another year to expel the Turkish forces from the north of the country and in October 1918 the whole of Palestine including what is now called the West Bank and Gaza was under the authority of the British Occupation Forces. The country was officially referred to as "Occupied Enemy Territory South."

Palestine was divided into thirteen districts, five in the south: Jerusalem, Jaffa, Hebron, Gaza and Beersheba, and eight in the north: Nablus, Jenin, Tulkarem, Haifa, Nazareth, Tiberias, Acre and Safad. In 1920, the number was reduced to ten and each district was placed under a British military governor with departments of health, education, finance, agriculture and public works. The military administration laid a complete system of government with departments of health, education, finance, agriculture and public work. At the outset of their occupation, The British military government's top priority was security, and therefore it was unable to carry out any program of reform in administration, taxation or law due to the hostile political climate and lack of administrative experience of the British officers who held the senior governments posts.[1]

On the 21st of July 1920 a civil administration took over, but it generally retained the administrative structure of the previous one. Besides the British High Commissioner as the head of the civil administration, the different departments were staffed with a large number of British employees including army officers and supported by a body of local staff.[2]

Palestine, along with Mesopotamia and Trans-Jordan, which had been under the rule of the defeated Turkish Empire prior to 1918, were placed under British Mandate according to the Treaty of Sevres signed between Britain and France in 1920.[3] The Mandate for Palestine was confirmed by the Council of the League of Nations on July 24, 1922. Article 22 of the Covenant of the League of Nations, June 28, 1919 entrusted the Mandate with the task of administering the territory of Palestine that formerly belonged to the Turkish Empire.[4] However, the administrative division and re-organization of the Occupied Territories in the first years of the British Mandate were undoubtedly designed to serve the strategic objectives of the British Government. One of these objectives was the establishment of a "Jewish national home" in Palestine in accordance with the Balfour Declaration of November 2, 1917:

> His majesty's Government view with favour the establishment in Palestine of a Jewish national home, and will use their best endeavours to facilitate the achievement of this object. It being

clearly understood that nothing shall be done which may prejudice the civil and religious rights of existing non-Jewish communities in Palestine, or the rights and political status enjoyed by Jews in any other country.[5]

The ten administrative districts into which Palestine was divided in 1920 were organized into three categories: A, B and C, according to its importance for the British; and the Jewish settlements which were concentrated in the northwest and on the coast were grouped under category A.[6]

The claim made by the British general command at the outset of the occupation that they would obey the terms of the International law and the Hague Convention and refrain from any substantial changes in the administration and in the existing laws of the Occupied Territories was invalidated by their far-reaching administrative measures and policies. The legitimacy of British administration in Palestine was predicated on Article 22 of the Covenant of the League of Nations, which "entrusted the tutelage of the inhabitants of the former non-Turkish provinces to advanced nations." However, the "Mandate for Palestine" document based on the above Article promised (Article 3) that the Mandatory administration would encourage local autonomy, but it fell short of mentioning any practical steps to be taken to achieve this objective. This contravened the spirit of Article 22, section 4 of the Covenant which stated that "certain communities formerly belonging to the Turkish Empire have reached a stage of development where their existence as independent nations can be provisionally recognized subject to the rendering of administrative advice and assistance by a Mandatory until such time as they are able to stand alone."[7] The wishes of these communities must be a principal consideration in the selection of the Mandatory." Furthermore, section 8 of the same article stipulated that "the degree of authority, control, or administration to be exercised by the Mandatory shall, if not previously agreed upon by the members of the league, be explicity defined in each case by the Council."[8]

Executive, Legislative and Judicial Administration

In 1922, the British government issued an "Order-in-Council" (a form of British colonial legislation) to serve as a constitution for the occupied Palestine, which embodied and articulated the articles of the Mandate. The "Order-in-Council" established the executive, legislative and judiciary authorities of the mandatory government. According to Article 4 of the Order, a British High Commissioner was to head the executive branch and administer the government of Palestine in addition to being the commander-in-chief of the armed forces.

The British Authorities in Palestine assumed their executive powers as soon as they captured the southern part of Palestine including Jerusalem in December 1917. General Clayton, the British political officer in Cairo appointed military officers to run the cities of Beersheba, Gaza, Ashkelon, Majdal, Ramleh, Ramallah, Jericho, Bethlehem, Hebron, Jaffa and finally Jerusalem, and also established a number of administrative positions covering the areas of finance, legal advice, agriculture, education, health, customs etc., and these positions were filled by both British officers and natives.[9] Other financial and administrative measures followed. The most important of these was the preparation of a yearly budget for the district *sanjak* of Jerusalem consisting of estimated revenues and expenditures.[10]

In retrospect, the administrative, organizational and financial measures initiated by the British in that period were mainly designed to serve the objective of paving the way towards the establishment of a Jewish state in Palestine. This was in accordance with the Balfour Declaration of November 2, 1917 in which the British foreign minister Lord Balfour promised the Zionist Federation that the British Government would do its best to facilitate the creation of a Jewish national home in Palestine. At the local level the British Military Government began to expel Palestinian employees and replace them with Jewish ones,[11] a measure that raised doubts among the Palestinians as to the real intentions of the Mandatory Government in Palestine. In 1920, the British High Commissioner set up an advisory council composed of ten British officials and ten non-officials; the latter were Palestinians representing the chief religious communities in Palestine: Moslems, Christians and Jews. The Council was to be consulted on questions of legislation and the High Commissioner was to preside over its deliberations.[12] The Council was later modified to include twenty members: ten officials and twelve non-officials in addition to the High Commissioner. The Council, however, was unable to perform its designated functions. A number of factors converged to weaken its role as a legislative body. These included the opposition of the local Arab population to the policies of the Mandatory with regard to the massive Jewish immigration, and more importantly to the confiscation of Arab lands by the British High Commissioner Herbert Samuel between 1920-1923, in addition to his decision to liquidate the Ottoman Agricultural Bank, a vital source for lending loans to Arab farmers.[13] The Palestinian representatives in the Council decided to boycott its meetings, and after 1923 it was composed only of heads of departments with no powers of legislation.[14]

The principal source of legislation remained the military orders issued by the British military commanders during 1917-1919 and later the laws enacted by the British High Commissioner of Palestine. In fact the Mandate document vested the powers of legislation and administration in the Mandatory (Article 1). This implied that the occupying power, i.e. the British would always have the final say in matters of legislation and execution, and this stood in contradiction to Article 3 of the same Mandate document, which stated "The Mandatory shall, so far as circumstances permit, encourage local autonomy."

With regard to the judiciary, the British launched a major effort to change the Ottoman judicial system that existed in Palestine before 1917 and replace it with one copied from the English model. The reorganization of the judiciary started as early as June 1918 even before the north of Palestine was occupied.[15] The process started with the establishment of a court of appeal in Jerusalem which sat as a supreme court, composed of three judges, with the powers to adjudicate in criminal as well as in civil cases. Two "first instance" courts were created to serve the districts of Jerusalem, Hebron, Jaffa and Gaza.

Special courts were created in areas which had no court of first instance and each court was composed of one British administrative officer assisted by a local judge and a notable or a British officer and two notables.[16] After the occupation of the north of Palestine, courts of first instance were created in Nablus, Haifa and Tiberias.[17] Religious courts, both Moslem and Christian were retained by the Mandatory. Other laws dealing with rules of procedure in both civil and criminal cases were issued by the Mandatory authorities.

The changes in the judicial system introduced by the British authorities in Palestine violated international laws on occupied territories which stipulate that no changes in the existing laws of the country under occupation should be made. The actions of the British in this respect would be repeated later by the Israelis after their occupation of the West Bank and Gaza in 1967. Both powers made changes in both the legal and administrative structures in order to achieve their political aims. In the case of the British Mandate there were two previously made commitments: The Balfour Declaration of 1917 and the Sykes-Picot Agreement of 1916 in which the two major powers of Britain and France divided the Near East between themselves, and Palestine with Trans-Jordan were to fall under the British sphere of Influence.[18] The judicial system in such circumstances assumed a different role than the traditional judiciaries. It became a tool for legitimizing the policies of the executive branch rather than protecting the ordinary citizens from illegal and arbitrary measures of the ruling authority.

Alongside the civil and religious courts, the British occupation forces established three levels of military courts to tackle security offenses. These were (a) the military court proper composed of three senior army officers (b) the military governor court composed of three junior officers and the military governor and (c) the summary military courts composed of one army officer. The courts were authorized to pass sentences of up to 5 years with hard labor and fines of up to 500 pounds on civilians indicted by these courts.[19]

In 1945, the Mandate High Commissioner issued a series of regulations called the "Emergency Laws" intended to deal with "special" situations like riots and demonstrations. These laws were used to help the British forces suppress resistance of both Arab and Jewish underground. It gave the Mandate authorities absolute powers providing for different forms of collective punishments including exile, house demolition for security offenders and extended curfews. The Israeli governments adopted the same emergency laws during its occupation of the West Bank and Gaza following the Six-day war of 1967.

Local Government and the British Administrative Policies Toward the Local Population

The Mandatory government attempted to provide some form of self-government through the establishment of elected local councils in towns and villages. The British occupation authorities kept in place the twenty-two municipal councils that existed during the Ottoman period. These were the councils of Acre, Beersheba, Beisan, Beit Jala, Bethlehem, Gaza, Haifa, Hebron, Jaffa, Jenin, Jerusalem, Khan Younis, Lod, Majdal, Nablus, Nazareth, Ramallah, Ramleh, Safad, Shafa-Amre, Tiberias and Tulkarem;[20] (Eight in the West Bank and two in Gaza). No municipal elections took place till 1927. At the end of 1926 a "Municipal Franchise Ordinance" was published deriving mainly from Ottoman sources.[21] Representation was to be proportional to the number of voters in each religious community residing in the town or village.

There are two points that are worth noting in this regard. First, there was a noticeable opposition by the Arab population to certain sections of the Ordinance, which rendered it ineffective. Second, Jewish settlements were excluded as they had their own independent local councils and suffered no interference by the British authorities in their internal affairs.[22]

The other level of local government consisted of the *mukhtars* (community headmen) and village councils. The number of these councils was increased by the Mandatory Authorities.[23] *Mukhtars* were common people who came from large families that owned property and usually were better-off than the rest of the population.[24]

The most significant development in local government came in 1934 with the issuance of the "Municipal Corporations Ordinance." It embodied already existing legislations concerning the formation of town councils, rules and regulations regarding voting, elections, and other relevant matters.

A critical examination of the articles of the above Ordinance clearly reveals the nature of the relationship between the central authority and the local government as envisaged by the British legislators. It was a power structure in which the local councils would be an extension of the executive authority rather than independent organs representing the true interests of the local electorate. To cite but a few examples from the above laws, Article 3 granted the High Commissioner full powers in supervising local elections choosing the date of elections, the polling centers, and selecting the people to supervise the voting activities. Sections 3,4 of Article 8 gave the High Commissioner the right to determine the number of each local council. The president of the local council (mayor) would not be chosen freely by the elected council members but he was to be appointed by the High Commissioner who also had the right to discharge him of his duties according to Article 50. Also the appointment of the vice-president of the council as well as the acceptance of his resignation fell within the jurisdiction of the High Commissioner according to Article 51. The implication of such rules projected a conception of the local mayor as an employee of the central authority rather than as an independent and freely elected local leader. Article 61 granted the High Commissioner the right to dissolve a local council if he so wished and appoint a new one or choose a committee to run local affairs till new elections were held. The above Ordinance established three levels of control over the local council: administrative, financial and legal. Section 1 of Article 85 made the appointment of senior municipal employees conditional on the approval of the district commissioner. Article 75 authorized the High Commissioner to determine the sources of revenue for the municipal budget as well as accounting and auditing procedures, whereas Article 77 required the local council to submit financial reports to the District Commissioner covering revenues and expenditures and granted the Commissioner the right to cancel or modify any item in the municipal budget, as he deemed necessary. Article 102 determined the kinds of municipal taxes to be levied and the tax rates applied. Other articles dealt with the legal controls of the central authority over the local councils, and although Article 99 of the above Ordinance allowed the municipal councils to issue by-laws based on the Ordinance, it specified the areas to which the by-laws would apply.

The above administrative and legal controls curtailed the powers of Arab local councils and diminished their role in the social and economic development of their communities. The situation was further complicated by the prevailing atmosphere of distrust that characterized the relationship between the Mandatory government and the Palestinian Arabs, which resulted mainly from the policies of the British authorities with regard to Jewish immigration into Palestine. The economic situation, especially in the period immediately following the British occupation of Palestine at the end of World War I and the inhabitants' poor financial resources and, consequently, their inability to pay taxes added to the difficulties which the local councils faced in providing the basic services to the citizens. Once again, it is evident that the British administrative policies in Palestine were designed to implement the stipulations of Article 2 of the Mandate document which declared that "the Mandatory shall be responsible for placing the country under such political, administrative and economic conditions as will secure the establishment of the Jewish national home, as laid down in the preamble."[25] The Mandatory Government seemed to ignore the second part of the Article calling for "the development of self governing institutions and also for safeguarding the civil and religious rights of all the inhabitants of Palestine, irrespective of race and religion." Furthermore, most of the administrative measures carried out by the British were viewed with suspicion by the Arab circles in view of the Mandatory policies regarding Jewish immigration into Palestine and the feeling among the Arabs that the Mandate did not provide enough safeguards for their national interests. Some local leaders even felt that they had more authority and self- government under Turkey than under the British.[26] This reflected how deep their disappointment was with the British Mandate. Till the end of the Mandate in 1948, the British administration remained basically colonial in character with key positions held by the British leaving only subordinate ones to native Palestinians.[27]

The failure of the British administrative policies to promote a truly self-government system for Palestinians could be attributed to a great extent to the secret agreements and commitments made by the British government to other parties notably France (Sykes-Picot Agreement 1916) and to the Zionist Federation (Balfour Declaration 1917). Any British attempts to promote self- government for the Palestinians in the mandated territories would have undermined earlier commitments made by the British to other parties and weakened the credibility of Britain among its allies whose interests seemed much more important to its global strategy than the interests of the people under its rule.

3

JORDANIAN ADMINISTRATION IN THE WEST BANK (1950-1967)

The Process of Integrating the West Bank into the Hashemite Kingdom of Jordan

On the eve of the British forces evacuation of Palestine and the creation of the State of Israel in May 1948, part of the land lying west of the River Jordan that had not been conquered by Israel (the West Bank) was in a state of utter political, economic and military chaos. The British armed forces had gone, creating a serious political vacuum, which was partly filled by a form of revolutionary administration under the rebel leader, Haj Amin Al-Husseini of Jerusalem, and partly by a cluster of Arab armies and volunteers who were pouring in from neighboring Arab countries. In the ensuing battles the Jordanian Arab Legion occupied the area extending from Jerusalem to Ramleh, the Iraqis seized the strategic Jenin-Tulkarem-Nablus Triangle and the Egyptians seized control of the towns of Beersheba, Hebron and Bethlehem. The Egyptian, the Iraqi and Syrian armies later withdrew leaving behind a land devastated by war with hundreds of thousands of refugees knocking at its gates. In that chaotic situation and after the issuance of the Barnadotte scheme by the United Nations, which proposed a settlement for the future of the parts of Palestine not incorporated into Israel, the Arab League asked the Arab Higher Committee of Hajj Amin Al-Husseini in September 1948 to declare an All-Palestinian government to be centered in Gaza. A congress was assembled in Gaza in the following month of October to proclaim the establishment of the All-Palestine Government.[1]

The membership of the Congress was drawn largely from all sectors of the population. It included presidents of local councils, representatives of the intelligentsia, tribal chiefs and members of national committees.[2] The Congress named itself "the National Assembly," elected as its head Haj Husseini and chose the members of an "All-Palestinian government." The National Assembly passed a number of resolutions including a proclamation of the establishment of a "free and democratic state in Palestine within the pre-May 15 borders and with Jerusalem as its capital."[3]

The Arab League recognized the new government while king Abdullah of Trans-Jordan fiercely opposed the move and launched an active political campaign to integrate the West Bank into the Kingdom of Jordan. King Abdullah proceeded to achieve his objective without hesitation. He visited the West Bank and through a joint effort orchestrated by pro-Jordanian elements in the area,[4] a Palestinian congress was convened in Jericho on December 1, 1948. The membership of the congress was composed mainly of tribal chiefs, mayors and *mukhtars* (village and community heads) under the leadership of a big land owner Sheikh Jaabari of Hebron. The Congress asked King Abdullah to unite Palestine and Jordan in a single monarchy and the King endorsed the decision.

The legality and constitutionality of the Congress of Jericho and its decisions have been a controversial matter ever since. Whether or not the delegation assembled in Jericho truly represented the population of the West Bank or enjoyed a popular mandate remains an open question. Those opposed to the move maintained that the composition of the delegation, the signatories of the basic legal document of the Union, were a group who formed a small and privileged sector of the population. They claimed that the leaders of the Congress represented big landowners and tradesmen whose main objective was to facilitate the traffic of their produce and imported goods through Jordanian territory as the land and sea routes through Palestine had been cut off following the creation of the state of Israel in the area.[5] Hajj Amin, the influential Mufti of Jerusalem, who enjoyed popular support, was opposed to the move, as were almost all Arab states. Abdullah's move "fell on them like a bombshell," and the Arab leaders condemned the action through the Arab League.[6]

The protagonists of the Union apparently took advantage of the chaotic situation in the area and the instinctive communal desire of the Palestinians for self-preservation, as well as the absence of a freely elected council of peoples' representatives to achieve their goal. Heedless of the opposition, Jordanian Authority in the West Bank was soon entrenched thanks mainly to the Arab Legion, which played an active role in consolidating Jordanian control over the West Bank Territory including East Jerusalem.

Shortly after the Jericho Conference of 1948, the political and administrative integration of the area of the West Bank got underway. However, due to the state of flux in the territories west of the River Jordan, the process was not completed till after the general parliamentary elections in both Banks in 1950. The membership to the Jordanian Chamber of Deputies was doubled to accommodate twenty Palestinians who were to occupy half of the seats in the House, and seven more Palestinians were appointed by Royal decree to the Senate (House of Notables).[7] In a period of two years the plans for administrative and legal integration were almost completed, and in 1952 the old local government of the West Bank was disbanded to pave way for the unification of the administrations of both Banks, which was to be directed from Amman.[8]

Executive, Legislative and Judicial Administration

The new constitution promulgated in the Kingdom in 1952 provided the legal framework within which the three integrated branches of government: executive, legislative and judiciary, functioned.[9] The administration of the kingdom was the responsibility of the council of ministers in accordance with decrees issued to this effect by the Council itself and approved by the king (Article 45, sections 1, 2). Administrative division of the kingdom, creation, organization and operation of the central government departments as well as appointment and dismissal of civil servants also were to be determined by decrees issued by the council of ministers and approved by the king (Article 120).

The kingdom, now comprising both the East and West Banks, was divided into eight major administrative districts called *liwas* or *muhafazas*, each under a governor called *mutassarrif* or *muhafez*. Each *liwa* was divided into smaller units called *qadas* (sub-districts) and these were further sub-divided into smaller units called *nahiyats* (precincts). A government decree on June 3, 1957 (Article 4) stipulated that governors of all major districts, sub-districts and precincts were to function under the control of the minister of interior of the central government.

The West Bank itself was divided into three major districts: Jerusalem, Nablus and Hebron. The *muhafez* or *mutassarrif* (governor) was the representative of the central government in Amman and head of the public administration and public security in his *muhafazah* or district. According to a government decree (Article 12, D) issued in January 1st 1966, the governor not only controlled all agencies of central government in his district, but was also empowered to supervise all local bodies in the area of his jurisdiction except the courts. According to Article 12 (B, C) of the above decree, the governor was called upon to cooperate with local bodies in the field of local services such as public health, construction, education and other social activities. The *muhafez* acted as a link between the central government and the local bodies. He was also required to submit monthly reports to the minister of interior on the political, economic and social conditions in his district in accordance with the same decree (Article 14, A).

Besides the *muhafez* there were two other important representatives of the government in the administrative hierarchy: the *qaim-maqam* (district officer) and the *mudir*. The *qaim-maqam* came after the *muhafez* in the administrative hierarchy and was in charge of the *qada* (sub-district). The *mudir* was in charge of a smaller area *nahiya* and, like the *muhafez* and the *qaim-maqam,* he represented the central government and controlled or supervised all government agencies in his area of jurisdiction, according to the above decree (Article 86).

Furthermore, the government decree of 1966 sanctioned the creation of executive and advisory bodies at the level of *muhafaza*, and only advisory bodies at the *qada* and *nahiyat* levels (Articles 35, 39, 67, 94). This arrangement, however, came at the end of the Jordanian rule in the West Bank and therefore it is not possible to give an objective assessment of their administrative value in terms of their contribution to administrative development during that period.

The administrative division introduced by the Jordanian government was not novel. It was similar to the Ottoman version produced by the reforms or the *tanzimat* in the middle of the nineteenth century, which were discussed earlier in the book. In assessing the role and functions of the executive branch during the Jordanian period, it is important to point out the following: First, the administrative system was highly centralized with the decision-making authority concentrated in the King and the cabinet of ministers, represented at the local level by the *muhafez* of each district who reported directly to the minister of interior. Second, the public bureaucracy suffered from a high degree of malfeasance, nepotism, favoritism and other forms of corruption, not to mention lack of efficiency. In a statement to the Parliament in June 1959, Jordan's premier Hazza Al-Majali described the administrative machinery as being plagued with nepotism, wastefulness and favoritism with many bureaucrats falling under the influence of certain sectors, who manipulated these bureaucrats to serve their own particular interests, while the rank and file showed very low morale and produced very little.[10] Third, political considerations, i.e. allegiance to the throne, played a significant part in appointments in the civil service despite the creation in 1955 of a civil service commission. It is also worth noting that the people of the West Bank, who constituted around forty-eight percent of the population of the kingdom in 1960 according to official statistics,[11] got only thirty-seven percent of the total number of classified civil servants, whereas classified civil servants from the East Bank provinces constituted around fifty-nine percent of the total number.[12] In brief, the public bureaucracy, like that in many other developing countries, served mainly the political and economic interests of the ruling elite and consequently played a minimal role in national development. Furthermore, district and sub-district governors were granted extra-legal powers in emergency situations. According to the "Collective Punishment Ordinance" No. 53, issued in 1953, the *muhafez* and the *qaim-maqam* were authorized to impose penalties including the payment of fines on the residents of certain areas who participated in activities detrimental to public security or causing damage to public property. Governors were also authorized to banish security offenders as well as common criminals and in less extreme cases force them to report to police stations daily or weekly.[13] It is not to be forgotten, however, that the Constitution published in 1952 cancelled all previous laws and regulations existing in the West Bank prior to 1952 including the Palestinian Constitution of 1922 (Article 129).

As regards the legislature, the Constitution of 1952 stipulated the creation of a two-chamber legislative body: a senate (house of notables) and parliament (chamber of deputies) (Article 62). Members of the Senate were to be appointed by the king while the members of parliament were to be elected by direct vote. Membership in both Houses was formally divided in half between the two Banks.

Formally, the legislative system established by the Constitution presented a model very close to that found in Western democracies, but in practice, things were different. The political environment in which the two chambers functioned was unstable most of the time, and therefore was not conducive to the flourishing of democracy. The kingdom faced a series of challenges and threats that aimed at destabilizing the monarchy. The governments responded by imposing more and more restrictions on the population, especially in the West Bank. According to defense regulation No.5 issued in 1954, the Minister of Interior was authorized to ban any public meeting, and order security forces to break it up in the name of public interest.[14] Other government regulations were issued in the successive year empowering the executive branch (represented here by the minister of interior and the *mutassarrif*) to disband existing political parties and refuse license to new ones.[15] The year 1956 was the only year in which free elections were held; and it was the first time that candidates to parliament were elected on party basis.[16] However, tension started to mount between the king and the cabinet and in April 1957, Prime Minister Suleiman Nablusi was accused of engineering a military coup-d'etat in collaboration with the chief of staff of the armed forces, and was dismissed.[17] A law was passed the same month, 1957 disbanding all political parties.[18] and was followed by massive arrests of opposition groups and leftist elements suspected of disloyalty to the throne.

Actually, the legislative system did not enjoy the independent status found in democratic states. Members of the legislature were not immune from prosecution and imprisonment. The executive branch headed by the king and supported by the army had the upper hand. Parliament could be dissolved by a Royal decree as happened in January 1956, and later in 1957 when the cabinet proclaimed martial law throughout the country and appointed military governors to execute the orders of the government. Additionally, both the convening and the closing of sessions of both Houses required a Royal decree and in emergency meetings the Parliament could deal only with matters approved by the king according to the Constitution (Article 82).

The legislative process was conducted in a non-democratic atmosphere, characterized most of the time by the absence of organized political opposition, particularly in the wake of the government's crackdown on political parties and the press, perceived to be hostile to the throne following the events of 1957. The poor economic conditions of the West Bank and the unbalanced growth between the two Banks, as illustrated in the West Bank's share in the GNP of the kingdom between 1960-1965 (36 percent versus 64 percent for East Bank),[19] reflected the failure of the parliament to enact legislations to improve the economic conditions of the Palestinians in the West Bank and fueled suspicions among the Palestinian population that they were discriminated against.[20] A report by the International Bank for Reconstruction and Development issued in 1957 found that industrial development was almost exclusively carried out in the East Bank and that the major industries, which employed large numbers of workers, such as cement factories, petrochemicals and textiles were concentrated in the East.[21]

The Judiciary

The Constitution of 1952 established an independent judiciary (Article 97). The court system was to be composed of three types of courts: regular, religious and special tribunals (Article 98). Regular courts were authorized to look into civil and criminal cases and they operated in a kind of a hierarchy starting with magistrates courts, then courts of first instance, moving up to courts of appeal. In 1952, the Jordanian Government issued a law (No. 26) according to which it added a court of cassation, sitting as the highest appellate court in civil and criminal cases, and as high court of justice it was composed of a president and at least six other judges with the authority to review the decisions of the courts of appeal and adjudicate in litigations involving citizens versus government agencies and organs of local government.[22] There were two courts of appeal, one in Amman, the other in Jerusalem, but the Court of Cassation was situated in the capital Amman. Another law (No.7)

issued in the same year authorized the establishment of "special tribunals" composed of military officers to deal with cases involving public security and espionage.[23]
The judicial system was probably the most efficient and organized of the three branches of public administration. This was mainly due to the existence of a body of proficient court officials including judges and attorneys who had been trained during the Mandatory period in Palestine. Nevertheless, the judicial system was not totally free from executive intervention and domination. Articles 124 and 125, sections 1, 2 of the Jordanian Constitution authorized the Council of Ministers to issue defense regulations empowering it, or any other appointed persons, to suspend existing laws and declare a state of emergency whenever the need arose to defend the country. Regulations issued in such circumstances as well as sentences passed by military tribunals could not be appealed or nullified in civil courts. In general the political environment, within which the judiciary found itself, did not contribute to the evolution of an independent and impartial court system.

Local Government:
Municipalities and Village Councils

According to Article 121 of the Jordanian Constitution of 1952, municipal and rural affairs were to be run by local councils in accordance with special laws. The Municipalities Ordinance issued in April 1955 provided the legal formwork within which these local units were to function.[24] According to this law the creation of a municipality was subject to the approval of the minister of interior in Amman (Article 5). The number of council members was also to be determined by the Minister of Interior (Article 7). Council members were to be elected directly by male residents of the town who paid municipal taxes within the municipal area of jurisdiction (Article 12). Duration of the town council was fixed at four years, but the Minister of Interior had the right to dissolve a council before its term of office period expired (Article 8, sections 1,2). A chairman (mayor) was to be chosen from among the councilors. The mayor presided over council meetings, represented the municipality before courts and official bodies and signed municipal contracts (Article 42).

The Council was responsible for performing the municipal functions which included among other things planning and zoning the town, granting building permits, regulating the use of water, electricity, sewage disposals, public markets, crafts and businesses, public transportation, providing for flood emergencies, and civil defense to protect the town from dangers. It also approved the annual budget, administered the properties and assets of the municipality and proposed by-laws, which regulated the municipal service (Article 41).

The Ordinance also specified the sources of revenue for the local councils, among which were the property tax collected by the ministry of finance and divided between the central government and the municipalities; customs, license rates, fees on auctioneering, rates on certain types of local activities and donations (Articles 46-51).

A close examination of the Municipalities Ordinance issued in 1955 would reveal that it did not represent any significant change in local government policy or attitude by the central government in Amman. The high degree of centralization and the dominance of the central government over the local administration that characterized the Ottoman and the British rules remained in effect. The Ordinance was almost an identical copy of the previous British and Turkish municipal laws. It incorporated the Turkish and British laws, particularly those articles designed to guarantee that the central government continue to have the final say in matters pertaining to local affairs. For example, Article 34 of the Ordinance, in both its original and amended forms, stipulated that "the Council of Ministers acting upon the recommendation of the Minister of Interior chooses a mayor from among the Council Members for a term of office extending till the end of the period of the council or till the council is dissolved." A similar stipulation is found in Article 51 of the British Municipal Ordinance of 1934. The same administrative and financial controls imposed by the central government over local councils were found in both the Turkish Municipal laws of 1877 and the British Municipalities Ordinance of 1934. A comparative analysis of a sample of articles covering the areas of personnel and finance in both the British and Jordanian Municipal Ordinances reveals an almost identical approach in dealing with local administration. For example, both Article 85, section 1, of the British Municipal laws of 1934 and Article 43 of the Jordanian ones make the appointment of the principal municipal employees subject to the approval of the District Commissioner (British Mandate) and the Minister of Interior (Jordan). Articles 42 and 53 of the Turkish Municipal Laws authorized the Turkish *Wali* and his council to determine the sources of revenue for the local councils. The British High Commissioner was granted the same authority according to Article 75 of the British Municipal Ordinance. All sources of revenue during the Jordanian period were specified in the Ordinance issued by the government (Articles 46-51) while local councils had very limited powers in this vital area. This kind of tight control exercised by the Central Government over local resources worked to diminish the capacity of the Local Councils to raise revenues not specified in the law. Thus in order to finance development projects, the Councils were compelled to seek financial help from the Central Government or depend on loans from commercial banks with high interest rates.

Village Councils

A law was issued in 1954 that authorized the creation of local councils for villages.[25] The creation of a village council fell under the authority of the Minister of Interior (Article 3). Duration of the council was for three years (Article 4). Membership to these councils was to be composed of *mukhtars* and the rest of the members to be elected by direct vote of the village male residents. The number of each village council was to be determined by the *muhafez* or *mutassarrif*, and the head of the council and his deputy were to be appointed by the *muhafez* (Article 5, sections 1-5).

Financial control was in the hands of officials appointed by the *muhafez* or *mutassarrif* (Article 16, section 1).

The functions and responsibilities of the village councils included the establishment of schools, public gardens, infirmaries, market control, health services, road construction, planting of trees and all other duties deemed necessary for the maintenance of public services in the village (Article 9).

As in the case of municipal councils, village councils were under the direct control of the central government and its representatives (district, and sub-district governors). The appointment of the council chairman, his dismissal, as well as the dissolving of the council, were decided upon by the district governors, and the council members had no way of appealing the decisions. On another level, the *mukhtar* or community headman exercised a significant degree of power in local affairs. According to the "Law of the *Mukhtars*" of 1958[26] (Article 4, sections 1,2), each clan in a city or village should elect a *mukhtar* from among its male members, and his appointment was subject to the approval of the *muhafez, mutassarrif* and the Minister of Interior, who also had the authority to dismiss him (Article 7, section 1). Article 8 of the above Law gave the *mukhtars* a wide range of duties and responsibilities. These included maintaining security in collaboration with security officials, assisting government officers in collecting taxes, reporting important incidents to authorities, keeping records and statistics and other civil duties. According to the "Law of Criminal Procedures of 1961" (Articles 7, 9), the *mukhtar* was considered to be one of the officials who assisted the Prosecutor General in implementing the authority of the justice officers.

The official status of the *mukhtar* in relation to both the central authority and the local community has been rather peculiar. Whereas the "Law of the *Mukhtars*" stipulated that he was elected by direct vote, his duties as specified in Article 8 of the same law focused on the security aspect of the job. This transformed his role to that of a security official rather than an elected representative of his clan or community. Local people perceived the *mukhtar*'s role as that of a government agent acting on behalf of the Central Authority.

Jordanian Administrative Policies in the West Bank

Jordanian administrative practices in the West Bank were designed primarily to implement the policy of integrating the area into the Hashemite Kingdom of Jordan. This political imperative was the principal determinant of administrative divisions and functions during that period. But unlike previous administrations, the Jordanian one was qualitatively different in at least one crucial aspect i.e. it was the first Arab administration to rule the area after more than four centuries of foreign rule. No less important was the fact that the peoples of both Banks had developed strong social, cultural and economic ties that could not be overlooked in forging any kind of alliance or unity between the two Banks. Furthermore, both Palestine and Trans-Jordan were mandated territories under Britain for quite a number of years and consequently shared in the colonial administrative heritage.

In order to reach an objective understanding of the Jordanian administrative policies in the period under consideration, one should be cognizant of the peculiar circumstances in which the unity between the East and West Bank evolved. The controversial manner in which the two areas were united gave rise to the problem of legitimacy, which was probably the principal factor in driving the Jordanian government to strengthen its grip over the local Palestinian population. Added to that was the volatile political and economic situation resulting from the Arab-Israeli war of 1948. Hundreds of thousands of refugees had been forced to leave their properties in what became the State of Israel and sought refuge in the West Bank and in Jordan. Their number in the West Bank reached 304,000 in the year 1952 which represented almost 27.5 percent of the total population in that year.[27] This placed a heavy burden on the evolving administrative structure and drained the economic resources necessary for growth and development.

The above, notwithstanding, Jordanian administration displayed a number of shortcomings reminiscent of the Ottoman and British regimes. Very little effort was exerted in reforming the archaic municipal laws copied en masse from the Turkish and British ones. Three laws can be cited in this respect. They are contained in Article 12 of the Jordanian Municipal Ordinance. Section 1 of this Article stipulated, "the eligible voter must be a male, twenty one years old"; section 2 requires that "he should be residing within the municipal corporate boundaries, at least twelve months prior to election day; section 3 of the same article added another requirement i.e. that the eligible voter must be one who paid a municipal tax. In view of the fact that in many towns only a small sector of the population lived within the municipal boundaries and consequently were not payers of municipal taxes and other rates necessary for voting rights, many town residents could not exercise their right to vote. In addition, the requirement that the eligible voter must be a male meant that almost half the town population was barred from taking municipal office. This perpetuated the trend that existed during the Ottoman and British periods that led to the emergence of city councils whose members in general represented a small segment of the population.

Local participation in the conduct of local affairs was in reality of secondary importance to public officials. A wide gap existed between the rulers and the ruled and, with the absence of constructive dialogue and dynamic participation, the people of the West Bank often felt they were ruled by an alien autocratic regime.[28] The poor economic conditions of the population, exacerbated by the sudden influx of hundreds of thousands of refugees, and the ensuing disruption of the social and the cultural fabric of the Palestinian community as a result of the 1948 War drained the already depleted resources of the public administration and had a negative impact on its ability to function properly. But despite the numerous shortcomings of the Jordanian administrative policies and practices during the period under discussion, four positive achievements are worth mentioning:

1. The Legislative Council created by the British Mandatory Government and composed of people appointed by the British was cancelled and replaced by a national parliament whose members represented the native population.

2. There was an indigenous national government that always included a high proportion of Palestinian figures and notables. The heads of all administrative departments were also drawn from the local population.

3. The notorious British defense regulations of 1945 ceased to exist.

4. There were sporadic attempts to reform the civil service financed by USAID and other international agencies that sought to improve efficiency through different mechanisms especially training.

4

EGYPTIAN ADMINISTRATION IN THE GAZA STRIP (1948-1967)

The Egyptian Military Government in the Gaza Strip

The Armistice Agreements signed between Israel and the Arab states which participated in the 1948 war provided for the Egyptian control of the Gaza Strip. The Egyptians assumed their administrative responsibilities in May 27, 1948 with an appointment of a vice-governor and a body of military and civil personnel to run the local affairs of the Strip.[1] The All-Palestine Government, which operated in Gaza in the few months following the war, was forced to leave for Cairo and the Egyptians became the sole rulers of the area.[2]

The Egyptian military governor of the Strip, appointed in 1949, assumed the legal and administrative powers and responsibilities of the former British High Commissioner especially those of the supreme commander of the armed forces, the chief justice and the head of the security, and the chief administrative officer.[3] Until

March 1962, the Gaza Strip was a military area under emergency laws and regulations. No political, legislative, or administrative authorities existed, aside from the Egyptian military governor.

The most significant development in the administration of the Strip by Egypt was the declaration of a new "Constitutional Order" in 1962.[4] It was probably the most serious step in ending the military rule and replacing it with civil administration. Unlike the law of 1955, which introduced only superficial changes in the political and administrative structure, the "Constitutional Order" of 1962 declared a number of sweeping reforms in the system. Among these was the creation of a semi-autonomous legislative system in Gaza through the establishment of the Legislative Council. The Constitutional Order included seventy-four articles that covered all aspects of life in a civil society as well as the functions of the legislative, executive and judicial branches of the public administration.[5] The new Constitutional Order provided for more popular participation in the decision-making process and theoretically paved the way for the emergence of a constitutional political entity. As for the composition of the Legislative Council according to Article 30 of the Order, the Egyptian governor was to be appointed as chairman (speaker) of the Council and that the Council should include the members of the former Executive Council created by the law of 1955 and which had been composed of the chief executives of government departments in the Strip.[6] This undermined the Council's legislative role as a true representative body of the people and curtailed its ability to act as a counterbalance to the executive branch represented by the Egyptian military administration. Towards the end of 1964, the Constitution was revised and 22 articles were added. The changes enlarged the legislative and political powers of the Council through such measures as forbidding the military governor from being a member of the Council, increasing the number of the elected representatives from 22 to 44 and decreasing the number of appointed members from ten to eight.[7]

The period between 1965-1967 witnessed the dramatic emergence of the Palestine Liberation Organization (PLO) and the constitutional struggle of the people of Gaza was transformed into a political struggle as the PLO represented for them the first sign of a possible realization of a long cherished hope of independence. The nationalist fervor, which swept the Arab World during the period added fuel to the intense feelings of the Gazans and other Palestinians. The PLO leadership, headed by Ahmed Shukeiry, established strong ties with the Egyptian government under Nasser. However, despite the initial successes of Shukeiry, especially the building of a nucleus of a people's army in Gaza, the actual authority remained in the hands of the Egyptian rulers till the War of 1967.

Local Government and the Refugee Problem

The first municipal council in Gaza was established during the Ottoman period in 1893, and the same council continued to operate till the end of the First World War in 1918. The British, upon their occupation of the city, appointed a new council composed of seven members to run the municipal affairs of the Gaza city. The last municipal elections during the British occupation took place in February 1946 and the Council remained in office till the Egyptian forces took over the strip in 1948. However, the Egyptian rulers continued to apply the laws of the British mandate with regard to local councils.

At the local level, three other towns besides Gaza had municipal councils. They were Deir-El-Balah, Khan Younis and Rafah, but these councils had limited authority and could provide only few basic services for their local communities. Among the other thirteen villages of the strip, six villages were allowed to establish local councils during the Egyptian rule. They were Jabaliah al-Nazleh, Beit Lahia, Beit Hanoun, Abasan Al-Gharibiyah, Abasan Al-Sharkiya and Khuzaa. The remaining seven villages had only *mukhtars* in charge of local affairs.

The role of the local authorities in economic and social development during the Egyptian period was minimal, especially during the first ten years of the Egyptian military administration, due mainly to poor financial resources and military control of the Strip. Also, it is worth noting that during the nineteen years of Egyptian rule, no elections for the local councils of Gaza and the other towns were held. The Egyptian military governor used to appoint both council members and mayors of towns in the Strip.

The first months following the 1948 War witnessed an influx of almost 200,000 refugees into the Gaza Strip. The number was double that of the native inhabitants of the area according to statistics.[8] The refugees sought shelter in Gaza and the surrounding towns and villages. Like in the West Bank, their presence put a tremendous strain on the economy of an already impoverished region. Taking care of such a number of dispossessed individuals was beyond the capacity of the few local councils which existed at the time. The absence of a viable government authority especially in the first months following the tragic events of May 1948 left most of the refugees in a helpless and nearly hopeless situation.

The refugee problem was not just an economic and social issue, but it was basically a political issue. Therefore, the Egyptian military administration in the Strip faced a dilemma in dealing with this problem. On the one hand, they had the moral and human responsibility to care for the refugees, but on the other, refugees could not be integrated within the social and economic fabric in order to get government services and benefits. And even if the administration wanted to extend its services to them, it did not have the means and resources to do so in light of the bad economic conditions prevailing then. On December 8, 1949, the U.N. passed Resolution No. 302 creating UNRWA: the United Nations Relief and Works Agency for Palestinian Refugees. The Agency commenced its activities on May 1, 1950 establishing an administrative apparatus to carry out its designated tasks particularly in the fields of education, health care, housing and welfare.[9] This international agency became the cardinal protector and provider of essential services for the refugees. However, its budget and human resources have not been sufficient to fulfill its mission adequately in the West Bank, Gaza and elsewhere in the region. In the meantime, other charitable and church organizations, both local and international, stepped in to help alleviate the suffering of the refugees and were able to provide some help in certain crucial areas like health, education and welfare.

With regard to Egyptian administrative policies in the Gaza Strip, we find a number of similarities between the situation there and that of the West Bank. The most noticeable was the fact that in both regions the decision-making authority resided in the Amman and Cairo and was oriented primarily to achieve the objectives of the central government. Both administrations functioned in a period of turmoil and uncertainty and suffered from severely limited economic resources. Nevertheless, a striking difference between the two should be noted: whereas the principal objective of Jordan was the total integration of the West Bank into the Hashemite Kingdom, the Egyptian Government considered its role in the Strip as a custodian and apparently was never enthusiastic about the prospect of integrating the area into Egypt. Nationalistic and probably economic considerations contributed to the adoption of such a policy. The result was a relatively more liberal attitude on the part of Egyptian administration toward the local population and their political aspirations, compared to the Jordanian administration in this regard.

5

THE WEST BANK AND GAZA UNDER ISRAELI MILITARY OCCUPATION (1967-1994)

Structural Changes and the Annexation of East Jerusalem

On the eve of its occupation of the land following the Arab defeat in 1967, the Israeli Government took a series of administrative steps with the aim of tightening its political, economic and military grip on the territories. These steps were implemented in a gradual but consistent manner irrespective of the political party in power. This raised doubts as to whether Israel was planning to annex the areas it occupied or use it as a bargaining chip in future negotiations with the Arab countries.

The process of re-structuring the administrative system started in the very early days of the occupation with the issuance of a series of military orders to this effect. Orders No.1 and 3 issued on June 7, 1967 transferred the legal and administrative powers vested in the Jordanian Government in the West Bank to the Israeli military governor. Order No. 3 established the security apparatus including the military courts and regulations. The first major step in the restructuring process was the annexation of East Jerusalem and the extension of the Israeli law to the whole city, allowing the municipality of West Jerusalem to incorporate the Eastern part within its area of jurisdiction.[1] This drastic measure was intended to change the political and legal status of the Arab inhabitants of the Eastern sector, making them Israeli citizens. Other major administrative steps followed. The former administrative division of the West Bank that was based on geographical factors was modified to adapt to the new Israeli policy in occupied territories. The most significant changes took place in the area of Jerusalem that had been reunited and administratively and legally separated from the West Bank. The areas surrounding Jerusalem that traditionally formed one administrative unit with the city, namely Bethlehem and Ramallah, were re-divided and became separate districts. Jericho became administratively attached to the district of Bethlehem. These changes had some negative implications for the Arab inhabitants of these areas for whom East Jerusalem was the political, economic and spiritual capital of Palestine. People living in the same geographic area suddenly found themselves subject to two different sets of laws and jurisdictions. The absence of geographical contiguity resulting from Israeli changes adversely affected both the local economy and the educational system in addition to the disruption of social and family ties between residents of East Jerusalem and the neighboring areas. School curricula and regulations had to be redesigned and resources reallocated to accommodate the new changes.

The Military Government in the Occupied Territories employed the services of 700 Israeli civilians, 400 in the West Bank and 300 in Gaza. These officials headed the major departments in which 20,000 Palestinian personnel worked, 14,000 in the West Bank and 6,000 in Gaza including municipal employees. Some of the public employees working in public departments previously worked under the Jordanian regime. The majority of public servants were schoolteachers. The major public departments were education, health, justice, agriculture, public works, industry and commerce, transportation, finance, communications, interior, labor and welfare, social affairs and tourism. Two major developments should be emphasized with regard to the status and evolution of the civil service under occupation. First, the system was under the absolute control of the Israeli Military Authorities. The military orders issued by the Military Governors in both the West Bank and Gaza provided the "legal" framework for the operation of the system. The most significant of these were orders No. 37, 367 and 368. Order No. 37 dated July 18, 1967 transferred the power of appointment formerly vested in the Jordanian Government to the Israeli officials in charge. Order No. 367 allowed the military authority to dismiss "staff for reasons of public order and the safety of the Israeli military forces." Order 368 empowered the area commander to deny any employee dismissed for security reasons any compensation or retirement benefits. The second development was the establishment of "civil administration" in 1981 that assumed the responsibility of the civil functions of the military government. Staff officers were appointed to take charge of different areas of civil affairs. This step was an attempt at an administrative division of functions between the Military Authorities subordinate to the Defense Ministry and Israeli civilian authorities. The aim was, on the one hand, to relieve the military government from its civilian responsibilities to enable it to dedicate more efforts to security matters, while on the other hand, the Israeli government could take a more active role in running the affairs of the Palestinian population in the Occupied Territories, thus leading gradually to a de-facto annexation of the area.[2] From 1981 onward, the Military Government operated on the basis of a double chain of command, one civil, another military.

The creation by the right-wing Likud government in Israel of the Village Leagues in 1981 represented another attempt to re-organize the administrative structure of the local government in the West Bank in order to create an alternative to the municipalities and village councils, which were suspected of being dominated by the PLO. The Israeli military authorities gave the Leagues both financial and moral support to help them overcome the opposition of the local population. Lacking legitimacy, the Leagues failed to provide a viable alternative to the local councils and were later abandoned.

Another dilemma produced by the Israeli policies in the Occupied Territories at the local level was the settlement movement encouraged by all Israeli governments. In the early eighties the Israeli governments started to allocate 300 million dollars annually for expanding the infrastructure for existing settlements and building new ones,[3] During 1982-1985 the number of settlers in the West Bank increased by 252 percent to reach 52,000 in 1985 from 26,000 in 1982.[4] By 1992 the number reached almost 120,000 in the West Bank and 3000 in Gaza. There are now over 250,000 settlers living in 143 settlements. The dilemma stems from the fact that Jewish settlements in the Occupied Territories formed a separate local government system that is not linked to the Palestinian local administration. In theory, they were under the authority of the civil administration, but in practice, they dealt directly with the Israeli ministries like other local councils inside the "Green Line"[4] (Israel proper). In other words, there were two distinct local government systems operating in the same geographical area with absolutely no kind of relationships between them. As a matter of fact, the existence of each one negated the existence of the other. This abnormal arrangement both undermined the status and authority of the Palestinian municipal governments and engendered conflict between the two authorities with regard to the utilization of water resources and the provision of services. There was no doubt, however, as to the preferential treatment accorded to Jewish local councils by the Israeli government at the expense of Palestinian Councils.[5]

The successive Israeli governments provided a number of incentives and privileges to Jewish settlers which included, among other things, free plots of land, low interest building loans, tax exemptions and generous government subsidies for infrastructure.[6] According to a well-publicized investigative report by an Israeli newspaper, a settler could get between 7-10 percent income tax reduction, a land purchase tax of only 0.5 percent instead of the usual 4.5 percent. Other privileges extended to Israeli entrepreneurs in the occupied territories included a ten-year exemption from income tax.[7] Jewish settlements received direct financial assistance from both the Jewish Agency and the Israeli Finance Ministry reaching 140 million NIS (approximately $56 million dollars) in 1991, in addition to the provision of security and transport services.[8]

The Military Orders and their Impact on Public Administration

The military orders issued by the military government of the West Bank and Gaza constituted the primary source of legislation in the areas. These orders, the number of which reached over 1342 in the West Bank and 800 in Gaza, covered almost all essential aspects that affected the livelihood of the people under Israeli rule. The orders went beyond the security needs of the occupying forces and were used as an instrument of political and economic control.

On June 7, 1967, the military commander of the occupied areas issued military proclamation No. 1 declaring the "assumption of authority" by the Israeli Forces over the Occupied Territories. The proclamations taking the form of military orders were not subject to appeal or review except by the Israeli government itself, which initiated them. Military Proclamation No. 2 "endowed the Area Commander with all legislative, executive and judicial powers" in the West Bank... and that "the laws which were in force up to 7 June 1967 shall remain in force as long as they are not contradicted by a subsequent military order." The Order placed the entire public administration system under the direct control of the military authorities. All the powers of government, legislation, appointment and administration were to be placed under the area commander, and exercised by him or by whoever was appointed by him to exercise that duty. Lawbreakers were threatened with severe punishment. The Occupation Authority granted itself unlimited powers in all executive, legislative and judiciary spheres. A number of laws that existed prior to June 5, 1967 were modified to adapt to the new policies of the Occupation. Most notable was the changes made in several articles of the Jordanian Municipal Ordinance of 1955 that were amended by a series of military orders to give more authority to the area commanders over municipal governments. Order No. 312 (1969) amended Article 36 of the Jordanian Municipal Ordinance. Order No. 331 (1969) amended Article 41, Section 1. Order No. 418 (1971), which provided the basis for the creation of the Supreme Planning Council, amended Article No. 5 of the Jordanian law No. 79 (1966), giving almost absolute authority to the Council in matters of urban planning and superseding that of the municipal councils and regional committees, which had an important role according to the amended Jordanian law. Order No. 459 (1972) amended Article 16 of the Jordanian Municipal Ordinance. Order No. 526 (1973) amended Article 42, section 10 of the ordinance. Order No. 537 (1974) amended Article 6 of the Ordinance. Order No. 632 (1976) amended Article 42, section 9. Some of these orders will be discussed in more details in the section dealing with the impact of "Occupation" on municipal services.

Unlike other forms of legislation, the Military Orders were not subject to review or appeal by impartial judicial authorities, and when at one time local Palestinian courts tried to intervene to stop illegal sale of land to Jewish settlers, the Occupation Authorities issued Order No. 1060 (June 1983) preventing these courts from dealing with such matters and empowering the Israeli Executive Review Committees to take up the cases of land transactions.[9] The Military Orders not only lacked legitimacy but were also a serious barrier to any positive or even normal development in the administrative system serving the local population. Also, they have not contributed to the betterment of the quality of life in the Occupied Territories. What they achieved was the transformation of the public service into an instrument of control and hegemony. Naturally, Jewish settlements in both the West Bank and Gaza were not covered by the military orders. They had their own book of orders and regulations and they were treated as if they were a part of Israeli urban centers.[10]

Local Government and Grass-Root Movements

Municipal and Village Councils

Twenty-five towns in the West Bank and four in the Gaza Strip had municipal councils. Municipal elections were held in 1976 that brought a new local leadership to these councils. The relationship between many of the elected councils and the military government was tense and laden with conflict. Several of the councils were dissolved while others submitted their resignations and were replaced by individuals appointed by the Occupation Authority. Officially the councils operated according to the Jordanian Municipal Ordinance of 1955, which the Israeli Authorities claimed was still in effect. In practice, the Military Orders took precedent in running their affairs. As mentioned earlier, a significant number of important articles in the above Ordinance were amended by a series of military orders, which either diminished their areas of jurisdiction or undermined the municipalities' role in community building and development. The issue of land acquisition has been the most sensitive one in this regard. The authority of municipal governments to plan and zone the land in or outside the city limits, was significantly curtailed by Order 418 (March 1971). The Order granted extensive powers to the "Supreme Planning Council," composed of people appointed by the Military Governor. These powers included the authority to nullify any municipal decisions in matters of planning and zoning and to forbid housing development within or outside the corporate limits of any town, even though an area may have already been zoned residential. It is evident that the primary purpose of the above Order was to facilitate the settlement policy of the Israeli government in the Occupied Areas.

Other amendments aimed at tightening the grip of the military governor over the municipal councils were in the areas of administration and finance. One of the earliest orders, 194 (December 1967), granted the area's military governor all powers previously vested in the *mutassarrif* and the Jordanian minister of interior over local councils. Order 312 (February 1969), amended Article 36 of the Jordanian Ordinance, making the acceptance of the resignation of a council member a prerogative of the Israeli authority (Israeli officer of interior in the civil administration) and not of the local council itself as Article 36 stipulates. Order 459 (March 1972), amended Article 16 of the Ordinance and granted the Israeli "Officer" the right to extend the period after which the list of candidates for municipal elections becomes official and no other candidates can be accepted. The reason behind the amendment was most probably the need of the Israeli Authorities for more time to convince people perceived to be more conciliatory or loyal to the Authorities to come foreword for nomination, thus creating more pressure on pro-PLO elements.

There were only 85 village councils in the West Bank and 7 in the Gaza Strip. Those of the West Bank officially operated according to the Jordanian law of Village Administration (No. 5, 1954). Villages without local councils were run for the most part by one or more *mukhtars* or headmen of large families. The "Jordanian Law of Village Administration" empowered local councils to carry out general responsibilities, regulate services and contribute to the development of the village. Similar to what they did to the municipalities, "the Israeli authorities used the councils as a means of controlling the rural sector"[11]

In 1981, the civil administration created the so-called "Village Leagues" to be used as a political counterbalance to both the Municipal and Rural councils. They empowered them with significant administrative powers and at one point it was almost impossible for a citizen to have any transaction approved by the Military Authorities without clearing it first through the Village League in his/her area of residence. The fierce opposition by the local population to these organizations de-legitimized them and they were finally abandoned as a viable form of local government.

Grass-Root Organizations: Objectives and Impact

During the twenty-eight years of occupation, it became clear that the administrative system created by the Israeli military government was deficient in providing the inhabitants of the West Bank and Gaza with the basic services at an acceptable level of quality, or contributing to local development. There was a noticeable gap between the amount of taxes collected from the Palestinian population and the quality of services provided by the occupation authorities. Taxes collected in the West Bank were transferred to the military government to finance its activities and little was directed for the improvement of local services or economic development in the Occupied Areas.[12] The system, in the first place, was not meant to serve the local population, but rather to help the Authorities maintain control over the inhabitants. Consequently, an alternative to the formal apparatus had to be found, and that alternative came in the form of grass-root organizations.

Over the years, there evolved a network of voluntary organizations in the Occupied Territories that sought to meet some of the basic needs of the population in such vital areas like health, education and agriculture. Most prominent among these were the industrial and agricultural cooperatives, medical help committees, social welfare and charitable societies, and-in the early months of the 1987 *Intifadah,* popular education committees. These organizations, with their limited resources, could not replace the formal government structure, but nonetheless, were able to provide basic services to the local population especially poor and low-income segments, which constituted the majority of the Palestinian people. Having relatively simple organizational structures, grass-root organizations were free from the cumbersome bureaucratic procedures, which normally afflict official bureaucracies making them ineffective in meeting public demands. These voluntary structures were more flexible and could adapt more swiftly to changes in the environment. This was particularly significant in light of the unstable conditions prevailing in the region. As a case in point, when the official school system was almost totally paralyzed during many months of the first *Intifada*, popular education committees that were organized on the spur of the moment and under dangerous circumstances, were able to fill the vacuum in this regard.

An Assessment of Public Administration in Palestine Under Israeli Occupation

The Civil Administration

Any objective evaluation of the administrative system, which operated in the Occupied Territories during 1967-1994, should take into consideration the political context within which the system operated. It was a peculiar form of administration that was primarily designed to serve the political interests of the occupying power while providing only the most basic services for the local inhabitants. Therefore, traditional criteria used in evaluation such as, efficiency, effectiveness, performance, productivity, economy and equity would seem irrelevant in this case. It is worthwhile, however, to point out some of the peculiar features that characterized the system during the period under discussion:

1. The system lacked legitimacy as it was an extension of the Military Regime that occupied the Palestinian Territories and consequently it enjoyed very little support from the local population.

2. The Public Service operated under two different sets of laws: Jordanian and Israeli in the West Bank and Egyptian and Israeli in Gaza.

3. The executive, legislative and judicial powers were concentrated in the person of the Military Governor and his deputies who reported directly to the Israeli Minister of Defense.

4. The Military Governor and all those officials in control were not accountable to any Palestinian public authority and the policies implemented by the Military Government were seldom subject to review or revision by any Palestinian individual or institution.

5. The two primary objectives of control and security topped the list of priorities to be attained by the system. The provision and regulation of public services that constitute the *raison-d'etre* of public administration in democratic societies were of secondary importance to the Occupation Forces.

6. More weight was assigned to the security record of the candidate for a civil service position than that given to his/her qualifications and technical competence.

Being designed as an instrument of control, the public administration's role in economic and social development in Palestine was minimal. In fact, it could be argued that it had a detrimental effect on development, given the numerous hurdles and obstacles that system placed in the way of generating sustainable economic growth in the Occupied Territories. Another shortcoming was the absence of a data base on Palestine that could be used for economic and regional planning; and the statistics that were available were misleading.[13]

Municipal and Village Councils

Local councils, particularly the municipalities, could have filled a gap to compensate for the shortcomings of the military administration in terms of community development, but, like the private sector, their effectiveness was curtailed by numerous constraints imposed by the Occupation Authorities. Local Councils, by virtue of their closeness to the communities they served, were more capable of understanding the actual needs of their constituencies and were in a position to provide solutions for many problems which the towns faced. But, as it has already been pointed out, these town councils often found themselves operating under the burden of the Military Orders and other official restrictions.

A major developmental function of the municipal councils, i.e. the planning and zoning of towns, was significantly weakened by Order No. 418 (March, 1971). Added to that, their limited financial resources, coupled with the stringent financial controls over the sources of revenues imposed by the Occupation have undermined any economic role that the Local Councils could play in the country.

Municipalities had two types of annual budgets: ordinary and developmental. The ordinary budget had fixed revenues and expenditures determined by the Jordanian Municipal Ordinance. The developmental budget, on the other hand, had to depend on irregular sources and donations including outside contributions. These contributions were subject to thorough investigations by the Military Authorities, and in a number of cases municipalities were prevented from receiving funds suspected of coming from the PLO. To make matters worse, the poor economy of the Occupied Territories weakened the tax base of the Palestinian Local Government, as many people were unable to pay property taxes and license fees, which constituted a significant component of municipal revenues. There were also complaints that the Authorities used to keep the municipalities' share of taxes collected by the Civil Administration, particularly the fuel tax, in violation of the "Municipal Ordinance" supposedly in force in the Occupied Territories. The result was that most town councils operated with budget deficits mounting from year to year. With limited tax revenues and negligible assistance from the Military Government it became increasingly difficult for municipalities to provide basic services, let alone initiate long- term developmental schemes. As an Israeli observer points out: "contrary to legends about the enlightened occupier, the large surplus that remained in Israeli hands from these taxes was not allocated for infrastructure development in the territories, or for the development of social services; rather, the surplus filled up Israeli coffers."[14]

The plight of the Village Councils was even worse. They too were used as instruments of control by the Authorities rather than being agencies for development.[15] The 85 Village Councils that existed in the West Bank operated under small size budgets and, administratively, were dominated by few individuals, mostly *mukhtars*, who represented powerful families and clans. Unlike Jewish settlements in the territories, village councils were not integrated in administrative regional councils, which could have contributed to their economic and social development efforts through a system of resource pooling and joint action.

The problems faced by the rural areas in the West Bank and Gaza Strip were overwhelming. Many villages lacked the basic infrastructure essential for the maintenance of a humanly acceptable level of survival. The majority had no electricity and running water, and farmers used primitive methods in agriculture and irrigation. The poor quality of life in these areas led to a large-scale emigration by the young and educated into the cities or abroad. Many left their fields to work as cheap labor in Israeli factories and settlements.

Lack Of Judicial Review

In evaluating the administrative system that evolved throughout the period of military occupation, it is important to point out the absence of legal controls or scrutiny over the civil bureaucracy by an impartial judiciary. Military orders constituted the primary source of legislation and they could not be repealed or appealed before a civil court. The Court of Appeal and the Court of Cassation that operated in the West Bank prior to 1967 ceased to exist, and the military order No. 412 issued in October 1970 invested the "Officer" in charge of the Judiciary with all the former powers and privileges of the Minister of Justice under Jordanian law. Another military order (No. 164 forbade the West Bank civil courts from hearing any complaints by local Palestinians or issuing any instructions enabling any one to submit a proceeding in cases involving the State of Israel, the Occupation Authorities and its employees unless the plaintiff(s) has a permit from the Area Commander. Military Order No. 129 issued in September 1967 gave the military the power to appoint, dismiss and promote all judges and prosecutors in the civil courts. The absence of an impartial third party to challenge the legality of the orders transformed the civil administration into a passive tool ready to implement orders without questioning. This not only adversely impacted the lives and the well-being of the local Palestinian population but also led to serious human rights violations especially as the Israeli governments oftentimes resorted to the British Emergency Regulations of 1945. These regulations, among other things, authorized the Military Commanders to blow up the homes of security suspects without going through a proper judicial process. Another crucial area that fell victim to the absence of judicial control and due process was land seizure by the military for the purpose of Jewish settlement. A series of orders to this effect has made possible the confiscation of large tracts of land in both the West Bank and Gaza. Some of these orders, such as Order No. 58, issued in 1967 concerning "Absentee Property," and Order No. 1060, issued in June 1980 concerning Law of "Registration of Immovable Property," amended the existing Jordanian Land laws and obliterated all legal obstacles to the expansion of settlements. Other orders facilitated the settlement process in more devious ways, like the practice of declaring certain areas as "closed military zones," (Order No. 388), and the restrictions on building and construction activities by the Palestinians embodied in Order No. 393, both issued in June 1970. Other vital areas also adversely affected were water resources and agriculture. Order No. 92, issued in August 1967, placed all water resources under Israeli authority, and according to Order No. 158, issued in November the same year, local Palestinian farmers were not allowed to operate or own water installations for extracting subterranean water without license from the Area Commander. Agricultural produce, the mainstay of Palestinian economy in the Occupied Territories, was also severely affected by a number of orders that restricted transportation in and out of the West Bank such as Order No. 47, issued in July 1967, while Israeli produce was permitted to enter freely into the Occupied Territories. The discriminatory nature of such orders was exemplified in Order No.1015, issued in August 1982, prohibiting Palestinians from planting fruit trees without first obtaining the permission of the Military Authority. The absurdity of this order is unveiled when one realizes that almost all Palestinian rural families grow fruit trees in their gardens.

6

PUBLIC ADMINISTRATION UNDER THE PALESTINIAN NATIONAL AUTHORITY

The agonizing development of the civil service system in Palestine following the Oslo Accords of 1993 embodies a unique interplay of conflicting political, economic and social forces that sought to gain ascendancy in the struggle for independence. Each of these forces represented certain vested interests in the yet-to-be born semi-state. The dynamics of the struggle reflected itself in both the creation and later development of public agencies that came to dominate and control the everyday life of the Palestinian population especially those living within the areas under Palestinian jurisdiction- classified according to the Oslo Agreements as Areas A and B.

The political milieu within which the new public administration functioned impacted both the composition and performance of government agencies. Likewise, but to a lesser extent, the non-government organizations network exhibited a similar tendency of allocating decision-making power based on the political map that existed in Palestine in the wake of the entry of the Palestine National Authority into the West Bank and Gaza. The immediate result was the emergence of a patronage system in which appointment to the executive and the judicial branches was made on the basis of political affiliation and nepotism. Public office became a kind of reward granted to those who belonged to the "right' political party, in this case Fatah, the main political faction in Palestine. Buying political loyalty, using government revenues, gave rise to different forms of corruption that had serious economic repercussions in view of the limited resources of the Palestinian entity that depended almost entirely on financial assistance from donor countries. One must remember, however, that the new government bureaucracy was not established from scratch and a significant part of its structure was inherited from the former colonial powers that ruled the country. Therefore, one may assume that some of the negative aspects of the new administration were part of an old heritage of colonial rule.

It would be difficult to understand the complexity of the picture without dealing first with three major issues that underlie any objective investigation of the administrative *status-quo* in Palestine at present. First there is the issue of sovereignty. Up to this moment no agreements have been reached regarding the final borders of the Palestinian political entity and the degree of autonomy it is destined to enjoy. According to the Oslo Agreements, the PNA was to be an interim governing authority with limited jurisdictions. It has full security and civilian control only in the territories designated as Area A. This area constitutes just 17 percent of the total area of the West Bank and Gaza. In area B that comprises 23 percent of the land, the Palestinian Authority is given responsibility for civil services while security matters remain in the hands of the Israeli army. In area C both security and civil administration are under Israeli jurisdiction. Under such complex arrangements, administrative organization for public services becomes fragmented and ineffective and the same population finds itself under different centers of control—a condition that is in total contradiction with a classic principle of organization—the unity of command. It would be naïve to assume, therefore, that the Israeli Civil Administration was dismantled and was replaced by a Palestinian independent authority. As a matter of fact, "the civil administration on the West Bank has continued with the same mixed tasks it has been carrying out since 1981."[1]

Second there is the multiplicity of legal frames of reference for the laws governing the functions and responsibilities of public agencies that exist in the Palestinian Authority. The three sources are the Jordanian law that was in force prior to 1967, the Military Orders issued by the Israeli Occupation Regime in Gaza and the West Bank between 1967-1993. In Gaza, besides the military orders, there were the Egyptian laws applied before the Israeli occupation. A number of laws were issued by the Palestinian Legislative Council and approved by the Chairman of the Palestinian Authority in the period between 1997-2000. They covered several important areas including civil service, firearms, elections for local councils, transportation, investment, environment, civil defense, organization of legal practice, arbitration, the handicapped, and local representative councils. There are many instances in which the above laws contradicted each other over the same issue making matters even more complicated for the ordinary citizen and the public official as well.

Third there is an almost total economic dependence of the Palestinian economy on Israel. A situation that has resulted from the many years of military occupation, during which, the Israeli market provided the livelihood for a substantial portion of the working sector—reaching 120,000 workers in 1999.[2] No serious efforts were undertaken by the consecutive Israeli governments to develop the Palestinian local economy. The West Bank and Gaza became a large consumer market for Israeli products. The Economic Protocols signed in Paris to govern economic relations between the two parties in 1994 failed to produce economic autonomy for the Palestinians, and provided little prospects for the possibility of economic liberation from Israeli economic domination of the Palestinian market.

The Legal Framework: The Oslo Accords 1993

Transfer of authority from Israel to the Palestinian Liberation Organization over the West Bank and Gaza was made possible by the Agreements signed in Oslo between the two parties in September 13,1993. The Accord was defined as a "declaration of principles." According to the Draft that was articulated in more detail in 1994 and 1995 an interim self-governing authority was to be established in the Liberated Territories starting in Gaza and Jericho first. The Preamble of the Agreement states that the legislative and executive authority was to be assumed by a Palestinian "Council" that will serve as an interim government for a transitional period not to exceed five years. As regards the Council, It was stipulated that:

1. Israel shall transfer powers and responsibilities as specified in this Agreement from the Israeli military government and its civil administration to the Council in accordance with this agreement. Israel shall continue to exercise powers and responsibilities not so transferred.

2. Pending the inauguration of the Council, the powers and responsibilities transferred to the Council shall be exercised by the Palestinian Authority, established in accordance with the Gaza-Jericho agreement, which shall also have the rights, liabilities and obligations to be assumed by the Council in this regard. Accordingly, the term "council" throughout this Agreement shall, pending the inauguration of the Council, be construed as meaning the Palestinian Authority.

3. The transfer and assumption of authority in civil spheres, powers and responsibilities shall be transferred and assumed as set out in the Protocol Concerning Civil affairs attached as Annex III to this Agreement (hereinafter "annex iii).

The Legislative Council

The Oslo Agreement stipulated the "holding of direct, free and general political elections for the Council and the Ra'ees (president) of the Executive Authority in order that the Palestinian people in the West Bank, Jerusalem and the Gaza Strip democratically elect accountable representatives. In January 1996 elections were held for both the Legislative Council and the President of the Palestinian National Authority. The Council comprised eighty-eight members representing sixteen districts: Jerusalem (7), Jericho (1), Bethlehem (4), Jenin (6), Hebron (10), Ramallah (7), Salfeet (1), Toubas (1), Qalqilya (2), Tulkarem (4), Nablus (8), Gaza City (12), Gaza North (7), Gaza Center (5), Khan Younis/Deir AlBalah (8), Rafah (5).

The Palestinian Legislative Council was mandated to pass laws specifying public policies that will be implemented by the Executive branch of the PNA. The mandate, however, was not extended to issues related to permanent status and foreign policy in accordance with the Oslo Accords. For this purpose the Council formed twelve committees dealing with issues pertaining to political matters, natural resources, education and social issues, Jerusalem, land and settlements, legal issues, the economy, refugees, security and interior, Council affairs, budget and finance, monitoring and human rights. The Council has dealt with a range of draft laws covering important political, social and economic activities but the President at the outset of the September 2000 uprising had endorsed only a limited number of laws.

The PLC has also assumed the responsibility of monitoring the performance of the Executive Authority through a number of mechanisms approved by its internal by-laws. A seventeen-member committee for monitoring performance and human rights was formed to carry out this activity. The Council was supposed to be dissolved after ending its term of office in 2000 but its term was extended citing the current political turmoil and the difficulty of conducting elections under the prevailing circumstances. Chairman Arafat, therefore, extended its mandate till further notice.

A critical assessment of the work of the Palestinian Parliament should take into consideration the political and economic context within which the Council functioned. The political and economic environment in Palestine during the last eight years has been characterized by instability and a high degree of uncertainty. But this should not detract the observer from citing a number of shortcomings and inadequacies that have affected the work of the Council since its inception.

1. The Council has not enjoyed the independent status it was supposed to have vis-à-vis the Executive Authority. This has significantly curtailed its power to pass legislation involving the actual demands of the public. It was very difficult to endorse any legislation not approved by President Arafat. The overwhelming majority in parliament were loyal to the Executive and belonged to the same dominant faction Fatah. "Those loyal to the Executive were docile to the degree that they abandoned their responsibility towards the Council and their constituency."[3] The marginalization of the role of the Legislative Assembly prompted a leading member and the former head of the Palestinian delegation to Madrid in 1991, Dr. Haider Abdel-Shafi, to resign from the Council in protest, according to his statement in a press release.[4]

2. The work of the Council's Committees has been hampered by the absence of an adequate data base and information system, needed in assessing and analyzing proposed legislations in a professional manner.[5]

3. The major failure of the Council has been in the monitoring and follow-up functions. This became apparent in its dealing with the General Controller's report of May 1997, which found that $323 million, almost 40 percent of the PA budget, were misused or wasted by government ministries. The parliamentary pressure led to a change in government but the file on corruption was closed and none of the suspects was ever

brought to trial. On the positive side, the Legislative Council was able to fulfill the role of a policy-setting body and succeeded in passing several important legislations such as the Law of the Palestinian NGOs, the Law of the Fiscal Authority, the Law for the Election of Palestinian Local Councils, the Law of Civil service, the Basic law and the Law for the Independence of the Judiciary. However, it took five years for the last two laws to be approved by President Arafat, (till May 2002).

The Executive Authority

The organizational structure of the PA executive is composed of three hierarchical levels: the president, the council of ministers (the cabinet) and the government agencies comprising both the civil and security services. The President, Chairman Arafat, was elected head of the PNA following the presidential elections held in January 1996. Arafat enjoys extensive and far-reaching powers, and he is the ultimate decision-maker in almost all civil and security matters within the Palestinian self-rule area. He is assisted by a number of political and economic advisors who wield influence on the political and administrative decision-making process.

The first cabinet was formed following the establishment of the Palestinian Authority in 1994. It was reshuffled after the first meeting of the Legislative Council on January 20, 1996. A third cabinet was set-up in August 1996. That Cabinet comprised 28 ministers of whom 20 were from the PLC. In September 2000 the number of cabinet ministers reached 34 as ex-ministers joined the cabinet. The choice of ministers depended entirely on Chairman Arafat. In theory, the cabinet represents the head of the executive branch, and in this capacity, it embodies the political control over the government bureaucracy. In reality, however, this role has been weakened by the excessive power exercised by the President over the government machinery, as will be shown later.

In response to mounting international and local pressure for democratic and administrative reform, the PNA President carried out a cabinet reshuffle in June 2002 that reduced the number of ministerial portfolios from 31 to 21. Some ministries such as the Ministry of Education and the Ministry of Higher Education were merged into one ministry, and new ministries were added, such as the Ministry of Natural Resources. The Security Apparatus was also reshuffled and a new head for Preventive Security was appointed. Two new ministers were appointed: one for the interior, the other for finance.

The Civil Service

A number of public departments and institutions were established with the formation of the first government. The bulk of the civil servants who had worked in the previous Israeli civil administration were retained and became part of the new bureaucracy. Thousands of people were appointed by the PNA in different public agencies by orders from President Arafat. By the end of 1999, according to a U.N report,[6] the number of employees working in civilian public institutions had reached 104,000. The figure includes all employees working in both the central and local government machinery as well as in the semi-autonomous institutions. In a public statement issued to the press, the Director of the Civil Service Commission put the number of employees working in the Central Government institutions in September 2000 at 57,000.[7] There are no accurate figures on the number of personnel working in the ten security organs operating before the September uprising, but it is generally estimated that their number ranged between 30, 000 to 35, 000 people in both the West Bank and Gaza. In addition to government ministries there are a number of public institutions performing important functions such as the Palestinian Monetary Authority, the Central Bureau of Statistics, the General Control Bureau, the Civil Service Commission and the Palestinian Economic Council For Development and Reconstruction (PECDAR). These enjoy semi- autonomous status and report directly to Chairman Arafat.

The organizational structure of government ministries follows the traditional model applied in neighboring Middle Eastern countries, most notably Jordan. The administrative pyramid of each ministry is headed by a deputy minister (Wakil-wizarah) followed down the hierarchical levels by public directors who head the major departments in the ministry. Administrative divisions, or departmentalization, is based, in most cases, on geographical criteria. Each department is divided into bureaus headed by bureau chiefs. It is important to note here that, in practice, both public directors and bureau chiefs are appointed directly by President Arafat without necessarily going through the ministerial channels or the Civil Service Commission.

Employment to other less important administrative positions as well as to other technical jobs must be processed by the Civil Service Commission and approved by the minister concerned according to standing regulations and procedures. Though the recruitment and selection process is ostensibly objective and based on professional criteria; in practice, it is often impacted by political and factional considerations. The President, for example, could bypass all formal procedures if he wished to appoint anyone in a public department.

The deficiencies and irregularities in the public service were disclosed in the 1996 annual report of the Palestinian General Control Bureau released in May 1997. The document created a public storm against the unlawful and unethical practices attributed to many public officials. In view of the gross violations allegedly committed by leading public figures in the PNA, a presidential committee was formed to review the report and present its recommendations to the President. The Monitoring Committee of the Legislative Council was also asked by the Council to review its contents and submit the results for discussion in the PNA.[8] The report of the PLC's Monitoring Committee, albeit critical of certain procedural mistakes of the General Control Bureau, confirmed most of the latter's findings and called for immediate administrative reform and rehabilitation of government institutions.⁹

Major Irregularities Cited In The PLC's Report:

1. Appointment to public positions is not made on the basis of professional qualifications of the applicant but depends, in most cases, on political patronage or other forms of nepotism.

2. Overlapping and duplicity in the work of many government ministries.

3. Lack of job description for administrative positions in the majority of public agencies.

4. Excessive number of employees in government departments causing a drain in financial resources.

5. Duplicity of decision-making centers especially in the Ministry of Finance which was split into two agencies: one in Gaza, the other in the West Bank, with each agency working almost independently of the other. There were also two civil service commissions, one in Gaza, and the other in Ramallah.

6. Lack of professionalism in recording and reporting accounts.

7. Numerous cases where the number of people holding top administrative positions in certain ministries exceed the number of those in middle and low administrative levels. The result has been an "inverted" hierarchical pyramid contrary to basic organizational principles and common sense. The Ministry of Information was cited as an example where 87.5% of its staff occupied top administrative positions.¹⁰

8. Conflict of interest where a number of leading public officials had equity shares in certain private companies that have business relationship with their departments

9. Absence of proper controlling and auditing mechanisms that insure a reasonable level of employee performance. This has led, according to the report, to a waste of resources and even to tragic loss of life in government hospitals.

A more systematic attempt to remold the Civil Service on rational principles was made through the issuance of the Civil Service Law in 1998. The above law included articles that dealt with major personnel areas such as appointment, job classification, promotion, separation, compensation etc. The job classification scheme contained in that law divided government jobs (excluding ministerial posts) into five categories or levels from the most to the least important. The administrative part of the Law was put into action while the implementation of the financial part was postponed depending on the financial status of the PNA. The new Law continued to uphold the privilege of the President to appoint the officials in the first category (Article 17), as well as the appointment of the Director of the General Control Bureau (Article 15).

A significant achievement of the above Law was the establishment of the first Civil Service Commission in Palestine that was entrusted with overseeing all major personnel functions in government (Articles 6, 7, 8). According to Article 6 the President of the PNA appoints the Commission's Director.

The Civil Service law was the target of criticism and its implementation was slow and arduous. The administrative-financial dichotomy created much controversy and constituted an obstacle in properly applying the law. The old pre-law personnel were adversely affected and suffered the loss of certain financial benefits especially with regard to promotion.

The most serious problem that has plagued the Palestinian bureaucracy since its inception has been the patronage system that became common practice. A substantial number of high- ranking administrative posts in both the civil and security services have been filled with persons lacking in professional qualifications. Government jobs have been traded for political favors and loyalty to the regime. This has had very negative implications for the performance of the bureaucracy. This practice has led to deterioration in both efficiency and effectiveness in the public service. Moreover, the use of public jobs to gain political favor resulted in an over-inflation in the number of government employees. Aside from the strains on the financial resources produced by bureaucratic overgrowth, economic and social development have been negatively affected through an increase in procedures and red tape that accompany bureaucratization. Restructuring the public institutions has become the most important challenge in the way of economic recovery in the wake of the devastations brought about by the military confrontations, and the Israeli incursions into Palestinian territories in the last two years.

Human Resources Management

Before assuming formal power in 1994, the PLO leadership had little experience in civil administration. Their functionaries were dispersed over many countries and their main activities were revolutionary and not administrative in nature. It was expected, therefore, that the newly established authority would rely heavily on the existing public agencies inherited from the previous Israeli administration. As time passed a growing number of recruits were employed in government service. Many of these people lacked the necessary skills and experience in public administration and it was obvious that there was a pressing need for basic training. Unfortunately, the Palestinian Authority had not prepared any systematic and comprehensive plan for human resource development in the public sector once it took power. It looked to the donor countries for technical and financial assistance in this regard. Local institutions such as the Palestinian universities and other NGOs were approached by different ministries to provide post-service training for certain categories of their employees, mostly those in middle management. The training programs, however, were sporadic and many of them were conducted on the spur of the moment. Training has not been based on needs assessment and lacked specific objectives. Furthermore, no follow-up has been conducted to determine the appropriateness and effectiveness of these programs. Surprisingly enough, many public agencies had no job description schemes or organizational charts, a basic requirement for personnel functions in large organizations. During the first two years of the PNA rule, an initiative to establish a government- training institute was made. The initiative came from the United Nations Development Program (UNDP) and meetings were held with different ministries for that purpose but the effort did not bear fruit for unknown reasons. The last two years witnessed a decline in the number and quality of training programs, owing to the violent uprising, and the destruction of many government institutions.

There are a number of factors that could prove detrimental to human resource development in Palestine. Chief among these is the poor compensation structure. "Compensation is a critical personnel activity because it symbolizes the relationship between employee contributions and organizational rewards."[11] It becomes even more critical under conditions of economic deprivation as that now prevailing in the country. In the education and health sectors the average monthly salary of a mid-level employee (schoolteacher and practical nurse) is around 250 American dollars. Inadequate compensation, and the absence of a viable incentive structure undoubtedly have a negative impact on the performance and job satisfaction of personnel. Regarding performance evaluation and promotion, the Civil Service Law issued in 1998, contained a number of articles that address these two personnel functions. Promotion is to be based on both seniority and performance. Employee appraisal will depend on yearly reports by supervisors. Copies of the appraisal reports are to be sent to the Civil Service Commission for review and record keeping. In spite of these stipulations that seem to be in line with advanced human resource management, promotions and employee appraisals are seldom carried out in accordance with the relevant articles of the above law. Political loyalties play a significant role in this respect. Another practice that is common in many government agencies, but highly criticized by rank and file employees, is the secrecy under which reports are written and submitted to higher levels, providing little chance for the appraised employee to discuss the evaluation report with his/her immediate supervisor.

Fiscal Management

This area may be characterized as the "Achilles' heel" of the Palestinian Authority. The main problem the PA has been wrestling with is irregular and inconsistent revenue pattern. Financial resources comprise an assortment of different items that are dependent on political considerations and ad-hoc agreements with the European Union and the United States. Before the introduction of the new financial reform plans, revenues came from a number of disparate sources. These included domestic taxes and tax clearances remitted by the Israeli treasury such as the value added tax and a percentage of income tax paid by Palestinians working inside the so-called "green line," as well as customs and excise duties collected by Israeli customs officials on goods imported by Palestinians through Israeli ports. Domestic sources included income tax paid by Palestinians working inside the West Bank and Gaza. A major source of income came from PA private commercial and investment interests inside and outside Palestinian territories. This source presented a further complication as it "has in some cases blurred the distinction between the private and public sectors, with adverse implications for efficiency and growth."[12] Monies received from donor countries, especially the EU went almost entirely to finance development projects. The situation changed somewhat in the wake of the September 2000 crisis, as some of these monies were channeled to cover the salaries of government employees after the Israeli government suspended the transfer of PA money held in Israel to the Palestinian Authority.

The expenditure side of the budget was no less problematic. Lack of viable financial resources was compounded with mismanagement and the absence of credible controls. The PLC "Reform Charter" presented to Arafat following the mounting pressures for reform in May 2002 referred to the fragmented decision-making structure in the Ministry of Finance and the many decision-makers in the Authority, who were empowered to spend money without passing through the proper legal procedures.[13] The patronage system, where large numbers of people were provided with government jobs as reward for political affiliation aggravated an already serious financial situation. The salaries and operations of both the civilian and security branches consumed about 70 percent of the annual budget.[14] It is worth noting that 29.15 percent of the operating expenditures in the 1997 budget went to the security apparatus while the Ministry of Education received 16.70 percent and the Ministry of Health 11.25 percent.[15]

The Authority also established and operated import monopolies and quasi-monopolies and other ventures that were exempt from taxes, such as petrol, cement, tobacco, telephone and telecommunications. The accounts of these monopolies were not subject to the regulations of the Finance Ministry.[16] A number of irregularities could be cited regarding public revenues. According to law, income from traffic citations must go to the Treasury as public revenue, but the police department in each district appropriated the money to be used for their own needs.[17]

On December 31, 2002, the newly appointed Minister of Finance submitted to the Legislative Council the first systematic budget proposal for approval. It contained a reasonable assessment of the financial situation in the PNA with some detailed projections of expected revenues and expenditures for the fiscal year 2003. What captures one's attention in the document is the minister's over-emphasis on financial accountability and transparency in dealing with public monies. He also reported the establishment of a national investment fund and called for a rigorous implementation of stringent financial and accounting controls in government.

In general, it does not seem that the financial management of the PA has been executed in an efficient and professional manner. In many cases funds were not appropriately handled. "There were violations and misuse of funds… and a lack of proper financial procedures."[18] There has been a very strong need for transparency and accountability in the area of financial management and control. Further, a number of leading figures of the PA were known to have equity shares in various commercial companies that have business contracts with government ministries creating conflict of interests.

Local Government

The West Bank and Gaza Strip were divided by the PNA into thirteen administrative divisions or governorates: Jerusalem, Hebron, Bethlehem, Jericho, Nablus, Qalqilia, Jenin, Tulkarem, Ramallah, Gaza, Gaza North, Khan Younis, Rafah. Each of these governorates was headed by a governor. The measure was taken based on an administrative order issued by the Minister of Local Government and approved by the President.

The PLC issued two legislations in 1997 regarding the establishment of local councils and the elections to these councils. However, no elections have been held since the PNA took over in 1994. In a number of towns and villages, heads of local councils were appointed directly by the Minister of Local Government and in others the previous mayors remained in power.

The Authority, after assuming control of the West Bank and Gaza, hastily introduced major changes in the structure and distribution of town councils. From 29 municipalities during the Israeli occupation regime the number jumped to 76 at present. Many village councils were transformed into municipal councils without adequate planning and preparation. It seems that these changes were motivated by purely political factors and were not made in accordance with a realistic and balanced developmental strategy, as should be the case in such instances. More importantly, the Local Councils Law contained a number of serious loopholes and deficiencies that need to be redressed. Contrary to modern trends that call for more decentralization of central government authority, the new law reaffirmed the old concepts of local government found in the old Jordanian Law of 1955 that was later modified in Jordan. A conspicuous feature of the above law was the omnipotence of the central authority over the local councils and the extensive powers granted to the minister of local government in regulating the affairs of these councils. The type of relationship between the central authority and local councils was described in article 2, section 1 of the Palestinian Law as follows: "the Executive Authority formulates the general policy to be followed by the Palestinian Local Councils and supervises the implementation of the functions and duties of these Councils, the organizational affairs of public projects, the budgeting process, the financial, administrative and legal controls pertaining to the areas of organization and regional planning in Palestine."

In financial management, for example, Article 21 stipulates that the local council would have to get the approval of the Minister of Local Government to obtain loans. The annual budget of the local council must be endorsed by the Minister before being implemented, according to Article 31. The Law for the Election of Local Councils authorizes the Minister of Local Government to decide on holding the elections and setting the date for their start (Article 3) and to postpone holding them for up to two weeks if the need arises (Article 4).

A critical reading of the law reveals the extent of the executive's control over local councils. This reflects the deep entrenchment of the old, but still prevailing tendencies of autocratic regimes in the Middle East, to keep a monopoly on power. The notion of sharing of political power between the central and local government is still far from being realized in this part of the world.

At the practical level, one notices the Central Government's hegemony over the local councils, embodied in the its interference in the affairs of local councils and overturning many of their decisions in municipal zoning and town planning. Despite the financial predicaments of the majority of local councils, they are prohibited from seeking or receiving financial aid from external sources without getting the approval of the Ministry of Local Government. Revenues collected by the Central Authority for local councils, and in particular, the fuel tax has not been transferred to the municipalities according to the Law.

As regards local representation, one should not overlook the fact that till this very moment, no elections for the local councils in the West Bank and Gaza have been held. Mayors and council members of these local units were appointed by the Minister of Local Government. Furthermore, internal rules were issued by the Executive "positing power in the Ministry of Local Government and the Governorates rather than in the local councils."[19]

Financing Local Councils

The Law of Local Councils issued in 1997, did not contain any significant changes regarding the financial structure of local councils. Sources of revenue and stipulations covering the patterns of expenditure were almost identical to those found in the Jordanian Municipal Ordinance that was in operation during the Jordanian and, to a certain extent, Israeli regimes. Local revenues continue to depend on property taxes, fees collected from town tradesmen and merchants on sales, as well as fees on crafts, industry and building licenses. Fines on traffic violations and vehicle license fees collected by the central authority. Fifty percent of these fees and fines are to be transferred to the Local Councils according to Article 25 of the above law. Municipal revenues also include education and garbage disposal taxes. A local council can receive donations and grants from external sources after the proper authorization. Central funding of local councils is referred to in Article 22.

There are two observations with respect to the financial situation of Palestinian Local Councils. First, revenue patterns continue to be highly structured leaving little room for creativity or innovation in seeking new sources of funding; second, the Central Government exercises tremendous power over the financing of local councils. As mentioned earlier, a local council has to secure an approval from the Minister of Local Government in order to obtain loans or grants from outside sources. The Minister must also approve any modification of the annual budget prepared by a local council (Article 31). Municipal financial reports and accounts must be submitted to the Ministry of Local Government for auditing and approval (Article 33). The stated purpose of this tight central control is to ensure financial accountability, but it is obvious that the Central Authority, like in almost all Middle-Eastern states, is determined to have the final say in the financial affairs of local government.

Tight financial control by the Central Authority, coupled with a weak tax base has worked to debilitate local government's capacity to carry out substantial development programs in Palestinian towns and villages. Local Councils have had to rely heavily on donor countries and international agencies for both financial and technical projects. Lack of a sustainable source of funding for development projects has reduced the role of local councils to that of maintenance and house keeping. Funds allocated for development are not normally included in the municipal annual budgets and appear only in separate documents labeled as " development budgets."

The financial situation has been made even more complex in the last two years by the deteriorating economic conditions of the people as a result of violence and conflict that have produced massive unemployment and other economic woes. The ordinary citizen has found himself unable to fulfill his/her financial obligations and pay taxes, and thus many municipalities have failed to deliver regular services and even pay their employees' salaries.

The Judiciary

In the view of many observers, especially in the business community, the Judiciary and the Court System have been the least efficient of the three branches of government. The state of the Judiciary under the Palestinian Authority has not significantly improved and most of the weaknesses that had plagued the system during the Israeli military occupation have remained. At the formal level, the Basic Law (constitution) issued by the legislative assembly stipulates the separation of the three branches: the executive, legislative and the judiciary; but practically, the separation did not materialize. The Judiciary did not enjoy the independent status it was supposed to have, and this has had adverse implication for its performance and credibility. The Law of the Judiciary, intended to introduce structural and manpower reforms in the system, took almost five years to be approved by Arafat. The process of implementing reforms was slow and in many instances court decisions were not enforced or their execution postponed mainly due to interference by influential members of the Executive Branch and the Security Services.

At the structural level, the system is composed of different types of courts. There are magistrates (reconciliation) courts, first instance (lower) courts, appellate courts and the Supreme Court. In addition there are military courts involving members of the Security and the Supreme State Security Court, which was established by a presidential decree in February 1995 for cases dealing with state security. Also there are religious courts: *sharia* for Moslems and ecclesiastical courts for Christians. The Court of Appeal in Ramallah, which has replaced the Court of Cassation and the High Court of Justice during the Jordanian regime, is authorized to hear cases aimed at annulling administrative orders and releasing illegally remanded or imprisoned individuals. It also exercises powers provided for under Article 10 of the Jordanian law of Courts Constitution of 1952.

The Palestinian Authority, responding to calls from the public and the local legal community, initiated some measures to restructure the system in order to make it more efficient and responsive. A new law titled "Law for the Constitution of Civil Courts" was issued in May 2001 and approved by the President. The Law provided for the establishment of courts of appeal in Jerusalem, Gaza and Ramallah, and one higher supreme court comprising two chambers: a court of cassation and a high court of justice. This action was preceded by another law constituting the "Supreme Judicial Council," charging it with full authority to appoint and discharge judges. The political turmoil and violence that characterized the years 2000-2001 stifled the implementation of these measures.

As in the case of the Palestinian Civil Service, the major problem in the Judiciary is the caliber of its manpower. The appointment of judges has often been influenced by nepotism and political affiliation rather than competence. The PA failed miserably in rehabilitating the system It inherited from the Israeli Occupation Authority—through the adoption of proper selection methods and training. A number of incompetent and corrupt judges remained in their posts leading to further deterioration of this important branch of government. The fact that the sensitive post of Attorney General has been vacant for many years is one of many examples reflecting the fragility of the Palestinian judiciary.

A devastating effect of an inadequate judicial system has been more keenly felt in the Palestinian economy than in other sectors. It acted as a disincentive for private investors contemplating setting up business ventures in the area under PNA jurisdiction. The poor state of law and order has not been conducive to the development of a normal business environment; and the concomitant feeling of insecurity on the part of potential and existing entrepreneurs led many of them to look elsewhere for starting a business.

The Socio-Cultural Context of Palestinian Public Administration

A public management system, wherever it exists, operates within a cultural milieu that defines its features and significantly shapes the behavior of its human element. Separating a public organization from its cultural setting is apt to produce a one-dimensional and distorted picture of the organization. Values, traditions, customs, mores, folktales and legends all converge to mold a particular or distinctive style of management in any country.

There is no doubt that the so-called rational model of organization that has been prevalent in industrialized Western countries was a cultural artifact as much as it was a technical response to the challenges of a developing capitalist mode of production. One could argue about the extent to which an organization, public or private, is an extension of the larger culture, or acts as a subculture, but the fact remains that the organization invariably reflects the basic value-system of a society. A shift in emphasis from one set of values in the community is invariably duplicated in the organizations existing in that community. Culture can also serve as a diagnostic tool in approaching many managerial problems especially in developing countries. In almost all societies culture is a major independent variable affecting organizational behavior at both the vertical (supervisor-subordinate) and lateral relations between employees working at parallel administrative levels. Among the cultural elements perceived to have a direct influence on the social environment of public organizations in Palestine are: distrust of authority, the primacy of family and clan, unbridled hospitality and a sense of fatalism.

Distrust of Authority

The negative and suspicious attitude towards rulers and persons in high places is a common phenomenon in the Middle Eastern societies that goes back thousands of years. A Jewish sage, Pirqe Avot, living in the first century B.C.E wrote "beware of the authorities, for they bring no one near them save for their own needs and purposes. They appear as friends when they are satisfied, but they help no man in his hour of need."[20] In reality, mistrust has also characterized the relationship between the rulers and their deputies. The Ottoman governors appointed by the central government were changed on a regular basis for fear of establishing a strong local power base in the provinces under their rule.[21] Centuries of foreign domination and repression worked to entrench this attitude among the general populace in this region of the world. It is worth noting, in this respect, that Palestine has never enjoyed an independent political status. External forces always controlled the destinies of the people and the country. A manifestation of this ingrained lack of trust is felt at the organizational level in the reluctance of many superiors to delegate authority to subordinates even in matters of small consequence. This attitude toward authority is almost universal among Arabs.

General Saad El- Shazily, a former Egyptian Chief of Staff remarked:

The alienation of the Arab people from their governments is frightening in degree and in potential consequences. The cynicism with which the Arab media are viewed is a clear sign of this. People in the Arab world expect their media neither to tell them the truth nor to standup for their rights. They have no illusions: the media exist to serve the interests of the man who is in power-no more, no less...[22]

The Primacy of the Family and the Clan

Perhaps no other societal structure is as strong as the family and the clan in influencing individual behavior in Arab society. Oftentimes, political divisions were drawn along family lines. Appreciating the importance of blood ties and kinship in the Palestinian community helps an observer understand why the practice of nepotism in public and private employment is hard to disappear. The patriarchal form of the Arab family is embodied in the narrow pyramidal and highly centralized structure of the organization. The office or department head projects the paternalistic image of a father dealing with his children. One way, upside down communication is the norm in Palestinian organizations. In the private sector, the majority of enterprises are family businesses. The owner of the business is, in most cases, the son or grandson of the founder. The sanctity of the family and blood-ties, more than any other factor, has made the problem of *wasta* (patronage) in Palestinian organizations incurable. It may also lead to a conflict of interest when a public manager is under family pressure to use the public office for the gain of family members and relatives. Kinship is a major source of corruption in Middle-Eastern government bureaucracies.

Unbridled Hospitality

This cultural value extends back thousands of years ago to the period when Arabs were living in a tribal society where many of them belonged to nomadic tribes roaming the Arabian Desert. Hospitality was not only a means of showing off, as it was a crucial tool for survival in an extremely hostile environment. No value was so glamorized in Arabic literature, folktales and legends as hospitality. The act of generosity is unconditional and is not hampered by any constraints. It does not recognize the line separating work from home. A public manager is obliged to entertain not only relatives but also friends and strangers in his/her office, serving them coffee and tea without having to worry about the time wasted on such social activities. Time-management is almost unheard of and could not be implemented even if the manager is under heavy pressure to set up a time-schedule. Hospitality is a high-order value that takes precedence over any administrative rules and regulations. Palestinian public managers trained in industrialized countries usually experience high levels of stress coping with such a cultural imperative. Work schedules are disrupted and even daily routine activities are halted in order to entertain a visitor coming unexpectedly to the office. It is considered impolite, in Arab culture, not to receive a guest even when it causes delay in doing one's job.

Fatalistic Mentality

Islam, which is the religion of the majority in Palestine, fosters a fatalistic attitude among the believers. Everything in life and society is pre-ordained by God the Almighty, and the faithful must accept God's will without question. The highly conservative and closed society of the Arabs has worked to solidify this type of mentality among the masses. The foreign powers that dominated the region have tacitly encouraged this trend as it was in their interests that the peoples under occupation submit to the will of the occupiers and believe that what happened to them was destined by God. "This powerlessness has had both material and cultural effects on their society and political perspectives. Various avenues to power and status have always existed but their scope and effectiveness has almost always depended on external forces."[23]

Translated into administrative behavior, vital managerial functions such as planning and forecasting have been negatively affected. Entrepreneurial spirit has been stifled and change has become even more difficult. Administrative reform is resisted not only by vested interests but also by cultural forces that encourage inertia and work to sustain the status quo.

Public administration in Palestine has also been impacted by other socio-economic factors such as a high fertility rate (one of the highest in the world), which places a strain on the ability of public agencies especially health and education to deliver their services in an efficient and effective manner. However, the trend has been offset during the last two years of turmoil as a massive emigration wave took place coupled with the displacement of thousands of people, especially in the Gaza Strip.

7

Issues in Palestinian Public Administration and the Thorny Road Toward Reform

Political Appointees

Politicization of public service is not a phenomenon peculiar to Palestine. It characterizes government agencies in many Third World States and, to a certain degree, some industrialized countries. In the United States, for example, a new president can appoint up to 2,400 employees in top government positions based on political loyalty.[1] Other sources estimate the number of political appointees to reach 3,300.[2] While the number seems to be high, actually its numerical weight becomes insignificant when matched against the total number of the American federal employees which is around two million. In Palestine, however, the number of people appointed on the basis of political affiliation is proportionately much higher than in many other countries. Though no official figures have ever been released concerning this practice, it is common knowledge that political patronage is rampant in the Palestinian bureaucracy. Political appointees also occupy positions in the upper echelons of the public service. Almost all directors general in the service belong to this category. One finds that political executives in the United States, though they enjoy important policy-making powers, are officially outside the civil service system and are without tenure. The Palestinian political appointees, on the other hand, are regarded as permanent civil servants that cannot be disposed of even if a new administration comes to power. Political appointees normally lack experience in public management. In Palestine most of them have not had a first university degree. The majority of them are former expatriates who were allowed back into the Palestinian entity following the signing of the Oslo Peace Accords. They were immediately installed in their positions without the proper preparation needed for managing a public office. The practice of filling top public management posts with people appointed on the basis of political loyalty is bound to have a negative impact on the efficiency and effectiveness of government service, as well as the tension that is likely to arise between them and career executives. It also diminishes employee accountability since political appointees feel no obligation to government and the only obligation they have is towards the persons who appointed them. The situation becomes even more complicated when appointment is done on the basis of political quota. In such cases, political directives of the employee's faction boss take precedence over orders coming from his/her immediate department boss. Superior-subordinate authority relationship becomes more problematic when, for example, each of them belongs to a different faction. A subordinate may not carry out an order or implement a policy if it runs counter to his/her faction's political interests. Regular rules and ordinary work procedures are sidestepped or ignored altogether. One can imagine the damage that can be inflicted on the efficiency and credibility of the civil service, especially when public executives are looked upon as role models by the general public. Moreover, political appointees, once solidly entrenched in their positions, become stumbling blocks in the way of future reform. Their accumulated vested interests will compel them to resist any change that can be perceived as threatening their interests and acquired privileges.

In undemocratic regimes, politicization of the public service has been used as a way of consolidating the power and authority of the ruling elite as well as a means of weakening the opposition by denying it access to the decision-making apparatus. In this way, politicization can impede those reform efforts that seek to make the bureaucracy more accountable.

Women in Leadership Positions

Despite the fact that the Palestinian family structure is paternalistic and male-dominated, the past three decades have witnessed an increasing number of women entering the workforce. This development came as a result of economic needs and the improvement in the level of education among women after many of them were able to join universities and other higher academic institutions in the late seventies of the last century. They were able to occupy positions previously closed to them and a lucky few rose to top management positions in the private sector. However, the majority of white- collar women employees in this sector took clerical, secretarial and other low-management jobs that are poorly paid. The situation in the government was not significantly different. At present, women comprise approximately 25% of the total number of public employees in the West Bank and 12% in Gaza. Palestinian official statistics indicate that in 1999 women comprised only 7.8 % of the total number of the top administrative elite of the bureaucracy.[3] In the Legislature there are only five women in the Council, which is composed of 88 members.[4] In local village and municipal councils in the West Bank there were only 11 women out of 3035 members in 1997. The number rose only slightly in the year 2000 reaching 53 out of 3277 members.[5] There are no female members in the Local Councils of the Gaza region. These figures clearly indicate that women are still on the periphery of decision-making circles in both the political and the administrative levels in the Palestinian National Authority.

Since there are no legal barriers, nor any political or educational constraints against women rising to leadership positions in the PNA, one wonders about the possible causes behind this state of affairs. The author conducted empirical research in the year 2000 to seek satisfactory answers to this question. Results of the study suggest that the main reason lies in the socialization process of women in the Palestinian family.[6] In the conservative Palestinian family, the traditional role of woman as mother and wife is deeply ingrained in the minds of girls since early childhood. Since public institutions are created in the image of a traditional family structure where the male is the dominant figure, few women have the chance to attain positions of leadership in the public bureaucracy even when there are no formal hurdles obstructing their promotion.

The majority of Palestinian women perceive work and career as an economic necessity that is incidental and transitory. It takes courage and perseverance to compete with male colleagues in organizations and therefore only a few can make it to top administrative positions. The male respondents in the sample did not express any explicit bias against women holding high administrative jobs, but their position runs counter to the social attitude in this respect. Most probably, male respondents in the sample wanted to appear courteous and open-minded.

Another social factor that should be considered in explaining the small number of women administrative leaders has to do with the fact that marriage and children force many women to stay at home and take care of their offspring. This, in a way, works to stifle her ambitions and efforts to rise in the hierarchical ladder of the organization. In the absence of adequate day-care centers and intense family pressures, women with children have little choice but to acquiesce and sacrifice their career for their families.

Notwithstanding the social obstacles, Palestinian women have been able to have their voice heard through a cluster of women's organizations and through mass enrollment in local universities. In two Palestinian universities—Bethlehem and Hebron—the ratio of female to male students is 3:2. With a proper and equitable recruitment policy the Palestinian Civil Service can absorb a substantial number of female university graduates in all public organizations.

Limited Sovereignty

Palestinian Authority operates under a limited political sovereignty. Prior to the current uprising, it had full sovereignty only over what is designated in the Interim Peace Agreements as Area A, which constitutes only 17% of the total size of the West Bank. In Area B, comprising 23%, the Authority is granted control only over civilian affairs. This situation has significantly curtailed the Authority's ability to provide needed services for the population. To complicate matters further, this political entity has no permanent or recognized borders, which is an essential component of statehood in today's world. With no clear demarcation lines of its borders, a state is unable to exercise sovereign power necessary for carrying out its duties and responsibilities. In Areas B and C, the Palestinian Authority has not been able to use its police force to maintain law and order when needed. In Area C, people find themselves paying double tax for both the Israeli Military Government and the PNA. The problem has been compounded by a variety of conflicting laws and military orders, some of which were enacted in previous periods. Service delivery and organizational performance are, without doubt, negatively affected by such an abnormal condition. When sovereignty is unclear and areas of jurisdiction are undetermined as in this case, any authority will find itself engulfed in conflict with other authorities over rights and privileges. Politics and administration are interlocked and an authority standing on shaky political grounds will not be able to fulfill its administrative obligations to the citizenry.

Moreover, a central authority with limited sovereignty has little prestige before its people. It is perceived as being weak and fragile and not to be taken seriously. Those suffering the most in such a situation are the civil servants who are in daily contact with the private citizens. There were many incidents in the years following the establishment of the PNA of people refusing to obey the law, or even taking the law into their own hands, thus creating an atmosphere of fear and uncertainty.

An important administrative function that is likely to be adversely affected by limited sovereignty, is the management of natural resources, especially water. The last few years witnessed continuous confrontations between the Palestinian Authority and the Israeli government over the right to exploit underground water reservoirs in certain geographic areas in the West Bank and Gaza. Since the areas occupied by settlements are considered by Israel to be outside the jurisdiction of the PNA, Palestinians are denied access to the water resources in these areas, resulting in chronic water shortages in Palestinian towns and villages. Limited sovereignty can also derail efforts aimed at building trade and economic relations with foreign countries since the Palestinian authority is bound by its other agreements with Israel, particularly the "Paris Economic Protocols."

The Role of Non-Government Organizations

During the Israeli occupation of the West Bank and Gaza, non-government organizations, foreign and local, played a very important role in providing basic services to the local population in several fields, in particular, medical care, agriculture, and social services, as well as funding and technical assistance for development projects. At a time when there was no national Palestinian Authority, non-government organizations and other institutions of civil society were viewed by many people and community leaders as providing an alternative source for social and economic survival under military occupation. NGOs also employed thousands of people thus helping mitigate the problem of unemployment in the Palestinian territories. Some of the foreign and international organizations, especially USAID, ANERA and UNDP spent millions of dollars on local community projects giving a boost to the economy. However, when the Palestinian Authority assumed power in 1994, donor countries geared part of the funds, formerly earmarked to the NGOs, to government ministries. This weakened the financial position of many NGOs and caused a number of them to close down. Furthermore, the Palestinian Authority started to regulate their activities and even to incorporate some of them into government ministries. The move was strongly opposed by the majority of the NGOs. They feared that the Authority was trying to place them under its direct control which would cause them to lose their independence. The Authority also made an attempt to create its own network of NGOs that would act as a counterforce to those organizations clinging to their independent status. This has led to more conflict between the two sides. Responding to both internal and external pressure, the Palestinian Legislative Council issued the " Law of the Palestinian NGOs" in 1997. The Law has provided the legal framework for the operation of these organizations with the goal of decreasing the on-going struggle between them and the Central Authority.

There are two major problems related to the issue of non-government organizations in Palestine. One is their unwavering insistence to preserve their independence. They resist becoming part of the official establishment for fear of losing their ability to make their own decisions. The second problem is related to the allocation of resources. NGOs feel that the Authority is competing with them for external financial aid. Many of these organizations believe that they provide better services than government organs and therefore should be given preference when it comes to financial grants from donor countries. The struggle over financial resources is expected to continue in the future irrespective of the passage of the above-mentioned law. In reality the conflict may intensify as a result of the weakening position of the Authority and the increasing power of the NGOs during the past two years of violence. Like many other Third World governments, the Palestinian Authority seeks to remain the central player in the "allocation of values" in the society.

The Thorny Road Toward Reform

The issue of reform in Third World Countries is one of the most intricate and the least understood topics in contemporary political dialogue. The history of administrative reform in these countries has not been a success story. Attempts at reform—to quote an overused phrase—"carried within itself the seeds of its own destruction." The dilemma of administrative reform lies in the fact that the very people who can make reform a reality are the ones who will most likely suffer from its consequences. For the privileged political elites in developing countries, reforming the public bureaucracy would inevitably weaken their hold on power and render them vulnerable to public prosecution once their "sins" are disclosed. What makes the issue even more complex is the lack of consensus even among experts and scholars regarding the definition of administrative reform. Different people interpret the concept differently. The objectives of reform, might also be different depending on the particular interest of the parties concerned. The oversimplification of the issue, by reducing it to a carrying out of technical procedural changes, has been largely responsible for the kind of fiascos the peoples of the developing world have experienced from time to time. The irony of reform in the Arab Middle Eastern societies, is that, historically, reform was used by the rulers to consolidate their power and make their control over the local population more stringent and comprehensive.

It is very important at this juncture for all the parties concerned to reach a consensus about the meaning of reform and specify the objectives of planned reform programs. This is the first and probably the most sensitive part of any strategy for administrative reform. Failure to reach a common understanding on this point will lead all efforts astray and will not provide any fruitful outcome.

Since the inception of the PNA in 1994, there were some international attempts aimed at reforming the newly established bureaucracy by streamlining its activities and organizing its functions in a more efficient manner. The earliest attempt was carried out by the United Nations Development Program (UNDP) in 1995. A team of experts were dispatched to Palestine and spent about 20 days studying and meeting with local experts. The mission submitted a report in which a number of important recommendations for improvement were made.[7] In June 2002, the Palestinian Authority announced a so-called 100 days reform plan based on the Presidential decree of June 12, 2002. The proposed plan included major changes to be implemented in the security, administrative and fiscal spheres. The measure was primarily designed to deflect calls emanating from both the United States and Israel, which accused the PA of harboring corruption and mismanagement of donor funds.

The highlights of the plan, according to the text published by Wafa (the official Palestinian News agency) on June 26. 2002, are as follows:

In The General Domain:

1. Reinforce the separation of powers, such that the legislative Council can play its role to the full, as well as the independence of the judiciary and the rule of law.

2. Restructure the ministries and governmental institutions, review their methods of work and create a modern and effective civil service as elements of a reform process that ensures the effectiveness and efficiency of work in the service of the citizen.

3. Prepare for holding municipal, legislative and presidential elections and ensure that elections are held within unions and organizations of civil society, wherever elections have not been held contrary to the by-laws of these organizations, thus reinforcing the principles of democracy, transparency and accountability.

In The Financial Domain:

1. Reform operations within the Ministry of Finance with a view to serve the public good and to enhance the credibility of the Palestinian National Authority in the financial domain, both internally and externally.

2. Deposit all income of the Palestinian National Authority: taxes, fees, profits from commercial and investment activities, foreign aid in grants and loans including finances extended to projects in a single account of the treasury, and implement the principle of the indivisibility of the treasury in the management of public funds.

3. Reorganize commercial and investment operations run by the Palestinian National Authority through the establishment of a Palestinian investment fund that will be responsible for managing all these operations and that will be managed by an accountable board subjected to the most stringent standards of disclosure and auditing.

4. Limit expansion of employment in the Public Sector and unify the payroll administration, placing it completely under the Ministry of Finance.

5. Finish work on a modern pension scheme and put it into force as quickly as possible.

6. Activate and develop internal auditing through the appointment of financial auditors from the Ministry of Finance in all positions of responsibility, and external auditing, by strengthening the independence of the office of Auditor General and having it submit regular reports to the president and the PLC.

7. Develop the process of preparing the general budget, including the development budget, through the establishment of an

organic link between recurrent expenditures and developmental expenditures.

In The Judicial Domain:

1. Activate the Judiciary and secure its needs, such as the appointment of the required number of judges and the building of court houses and offices of the district attorneys in the various cities, as well as building modern prison facilities.

2. Implement measures required by the "Judiciary law," which went into force on 18 June 2002, such as the formation of the Court of Cassation, the establishment of "Department of Judicial Inspection," and the modernization and development of court administrations.

3. Prepare draft laws, decrees and decisions that will be required once the "Basic law" goes into effect.

4. Establish the "Governmental Legal Cases Administration," which will handle legal cases to which the Government is party.

There were also other measures to be implemented in some important areas such as civil society institutions, education and security apparatuses. The Authority committed itself to start putting these measures into force within a very short period of time. Recently, Chairman Arafat, bowing to pressure from the United States and the "Quartet" agreed to appoint a prime minister to head the Palestinian Council of Ministers.

The important question is: will the announced reforms produce the expected results? Politics aside, an objective diagnosis of the current malaise in Palestinian administration reveals a number of idiosyncrasies. The public bureaucracy in Palestine is characterized by two abnormal and intertwined phenomena. These are the dualism and rivalry between "parallel authorities." At the national level, major policy issues have been decided by two representative bodies: the National Council and the Legislative Assembly. Members of the former are appointed by Arafat, whereby political factions are represented on the basis of a quota system. The members of the latter were elected in the general elections in the West Bank and Gaza in 1996. While the Legislative Assembly represents Palestinians living inside the West Bank and Gaza, the National Council is an all-embracing body that is supposed to represent Palestinians in the Diaspora as well as those residing in the areas under the Palestinian National Authority. The two bodies have not often been in agreement over national policies and each one claims to have more legitimacy than the other. Parallelism, at the level of ministries, was confirmed by a Palestinian minister:

> ... in the past stage there were needless establishments parallel to the ministries. There were ministries with intertwined duties and activities, which confused citizens, donor international institutions and foreign diplomacy. Sometimes there were rivalry or repugnance between those ministries. There are many examples, such as the Housing Ministry, the Public Works Ministry, and the Palestinian Economic Council For Development and Reconstruction.[8]

At the local level, one finds a similar dualism and rivalry existing between governors and municipal authorities in determining crucial issues, leading in many instances to inter-organizational conflicts and friction. Nowhere was the phenomenon more evident than in the security apparatuses where different agencies encroached on the jurisdictions of each other creating a sense of confusion and disorientation among the populace. Dualism and rivalry also characterized the work of the Civil Service when two civil service commissions operated independently in both the West Bank and Gaza for a number of years before being merged into one organization.

Reform efforts have also been blocked by the over-concentration of power in the Chairman of the Authority, Yasser Arafat. It has been difficult for any government agency to carry out substantial reform plans without first getting his approval, since any funding for such plans must be endorsed by him. In the opinion of a legislative council member, "there is only one Institution, the Presidency and only Arafat knows how the budget is managed"[9]. The Chairman's word overrules any decision taken by a bureaucrat irrespective of the administrative status that the official enjoys. There were many instances where people were appointed in government agencies by direct orders from Arafat even though no vacancies were available, and the agency's director general was not consulted prior to their appointment.

Another peculiar feature of the Palestinian public service is the so-called "insider versus outsider" status in the service. This refers to the composition of manpower in the civil bureaucracy and in the security apparatuses. Insiders refer to employees from the West Bank and Gaza while outsiders refer to Palestinians who were brought by Arafat from exile and were given residency status in Palestine in accordance with the Oslo Agreements. Though both groups are Palestinians and share in the same values and aspirations, each group has a different background and political experience. Most of those coming from the Diaspora had a military background and were trained as militia fighters. Nonetheless, a great number of them were offered leading positions in the bureaucracy, giving rise to suspicions as to the technical competence of the "outsiders."

This uneasy situation has been created by a feeling of obligation on the part of Arafat and the Authority that all those who fought against Israel were entitled to government positions, even if they were not qualified or inadequately equipped to manage high level administrative positions.

Impediments to reform are not exclusively subjective. In other words, they do not emanate solely from those who run the system. There are objective factors that are social and cultural in nature and can be found in other Arab countries. The most prominent of which is *wasta* (nepotism). In the Middle East, family ties and interpersonal relationships play a significant role in selection for jobs in both the private and public sectors. In Palestine, kinship is considered by many to be even more powerful than political affiliation in influencing an individuals' behavior. This phenomenon has been widely studied and thoroughly researched in past years in light of its great impact on administrative performance in this part of the world. The practice is so deeply entrenched in Arab organizations that it has resisted all kinds of measures to eliminate or even bring it under control.

A major stumbling block in the way of effective administrative reform is undoubtedly the political situation in the Occupied Territories that has been plagued by instability and violence especially during the last two years. A number of government and civil society institutions have been damaged, some irreparably, by Israeli military incursions into Palestinian towns. The absence of a strong organized opposition may also contribute to the continuation of the status quo, at least for the near future. It is an established fact that programs for reform need a strong political backing in order to succeed. Political will is crucial and the lack of it means a death certificate for any serious reform programs. Reforms carried out without the ruling political circles lending it the necessary support would be reduced to cosmetic changes. A program for reform should be a comprehensive one that involves the three branches of government: executive, legislative and judicial. Only an integrated and strategic approach can yield positive results.

8

Conclusions

The government in Palestine as well as in many other parts of the globe is the principal employer of manpower and the provider of essential public services. The role of public administration in fostering economic growth, especially in developing countries is crucial. In light of the fragility of the private sector and the increasing needs for regulation in an ever-changing environment of globalization, an inefficient state administration can be an impediment to economic prosperity. Poor performance of government agencies negatively impacts the private sector with serious repercussions for the economy. The role of government bureaucracy in economic development in Palestine has been hampered by various constraints. The most serious of which has been the absence of a democratic tradition that emphasizes separation of powers and a system of checks and balances. This has encouraged the political usurpation of the public administration, using it as a tool of control and domination. Therefore, any future development of the public administration is contingent upon changes in the political structure of the National Authority. The political setting envisaged for a proper functioning of an effective public service should be based on the concept of a free and democratically elected government representing the true interests of the people.

The study has traced the evolution of the public administration in Palestine since the middle of the 19th century when the reforms, known as the *tanzimat* marked the beginning of a "westernization" process ostensibly aimed at modernizing the Ottoman Empire. Subsequent developments, however, revealed the failure of these reforms to create a genuine system of local government in the provinces ruled by the Ottoman Turks, including Palestine, which administratively was part of "Greater" Syria. While the new administrative arrangements were primarily intended to placate the European Powers, they actually helped the central authority in Constantinople by facilitating its control over the populations and expediting the collection of taxes. Local administration played no significant role in the social and economic development of Palestine and when the Ottoman Turks left Palestine after their defeat in 1917, the country was in utter poverty and deprivation.

The British administration that followed the Ottomans introduced some changes especially in the municipal services. But their overriding concern was to prepare the ground for the establishment of a Jewish national home in Palestine based on their commitments to the Zionist Federation spelled out in the Balfour Declaration. Therefore, their administrative policies in that area were both directly and indirectly linked to that political objective. The British Mandate made some improvements in the administration of the country, modernizing its infrastructure and developing its health and education systems, but in essence it was a colonial regime that lacked legitimacy and popularity. The incessant political turmoil that engulfed the country during most of the British reign worked to offset any advantages gained by the local population in terms of economic and social development.

The War of 1948 marked a turning point in the modern history of Palestine. The new Jewish State incorporated most of historical Palestine, and the rest was integrated into the Kingdom of Jordan and became known as the West Bank. Gaza was left under Egyptian control. Both the West Bank and Gaza remained in that position till the 1967 War. As the Jordanian government extended its sovereignty over the West Bank, it proceeded to restructure the public bureaucracy in order to facilitate the process of unification. It was no easy task in view of the tremendous obstacles and challenges that lay ahead. The volatile political situation of the kingdom in addition to poor economic conditions and weak civil society institutions all converged to produce an inefficient and corrupt public administration during that period. The system was monopolized by the ruling elites and served as a means of control rather than a catalyst for social and economic development. The limited reforms sponsored and financed by international agencies produced little results and only superficial changes in the structure and performance of government agencies. Egyptian control of Gaza was less stringent owing to objective factors and a more sympathetic attitude on the part of Nasserite governments in Cairo towards the Palestinian nationalistic aspirations for independence. But in both cases, the two systems were highly centralized and the decision-making power was in the hands of the Jordanian and Egyptian authorities.

With the occupation of the West Bank and Gaza by the Israeli army following the June War of 1967, the Palestinian Territories entered a new phase of political struggle that had a far-reaching impact on the economy and the social fabric of the population. The challenge was much more serious and dramatic than before. For the third time in their modern history, the Palestinians were subject to foreign domination, but unlike previous ones, this time the people perceived the occupation to be more dangerous because of the settlement policies adopted by successive Israeli governments. These settlements created new facts on the ground and diminished the prospects of developing the Palestinian Territories into an independent and self-sustained political and economic entity. Similar to the colonial administrations before, the Occupying Power established a public administration system that served its political and economic purposes, while providing a minimal level of basic services to the local population. The Occupation Forces used military orders as the "legal" base for the implementation of their policies. Through these orders, Israel was able to annul and modify pre-existing laws and regulations that had governed the daily lives of the Palestinian public under previous regimes. Local councils enjoyed a relatively more independence than central government agencies in running the local affairs, but their role in economic and social development was insignificant in view of the restrictions imposed by the military authorities, especially in the areas of funding and zoning. International organizations and foreign countries particularly the European Community funded almost all the development projects carried out by municipal governments in the West Bank and Gaza. Non-government organizations played an important function in providing some vital services to the public such as health, education and agriculture.

The Oslo Accords signed in 1993 between Israel and the PLO was supposed to mark the end of the occupation and the start of a new phase in the relationship between the two antagonists that would eventually lead to Palestinian independence. The transitional Palestinian Authority created by these agreements took over most of the civil and security responsibilities formerly exercised by the Israeli Military Authorities in the West Bank and Gaza. However, the PA functioned under limited sovereignty, and this has curtailed its ability to function in a normal and effective manner. Nonetheless, it could have brought enormous improvements in the plight of the Palestinian citizens despite the restrictions and challenges facing it had it not embarked on an archaic style of governance that was reminiscent of old epochs. One of the most disturbing practices was the Authority's reliance on a form of "spoils system" in the recruitment of public officials, who were mostly chosen for their political and family ties rather than their competence. Financial irregularities, lack of accountability and fiscal mismanagement negatively impacted the evolving economy and discouraged investment by private entrepreneurs that was badly needed in the country. Once again, one finds the same scenario repeating itself. Public administration was being usurped for the purpose of political control rather than as a means of facilitating and encouraging economic and social development.

In light of the poor performance and mismanagement reported in a good number of public agencies, a comprehensive strategy for human resource development is in order. Training should be a continuous process and not carried out just in response to the demands of foreign donors. A central government agency for training and development of government personnel is urgently needed. It can play a vital role in improving the quality of public service and in preparing the Palestinian bureaucracy for the challenges of globalization.

There has been a flood of complaints voiced by both civil society organizations and private individuals regarding alleged abuses of authority and corruption among senior public officials during the past few years. It might be timely and appropriate, therefore, to consider the establishment of a form of ombudsman that can look into such complaints and allegations. This organization should be independent and free from any interference by the executive authority. The urgency of such a body cannot be overestimated in view of the weakness and inadequacy of the Judiciary, which may need several more years to ascertain its role as a guardian of human rights in Palestine.

Another important issue that must be addressed in any future reform plans is the status of women in the public bureaucracy. This vital sector of the population is not adequately represented in the middle and upper echelons of the Palestinian Authority. The government must take the initiative to elevate the status of women in public agencies. There are a number of measures that the Authority can take in this respect. One recommended measure is to adopt a quota system of proportional representation based on the fact that women comprise half the population in the Palestinian society. Many are highly educated and can, if properly trained, take positions of leadership in the civil service thereby enriching and enhancing government productivity.

The development of a viable and effective government apparatus cannot proceed without investing in the human element, which is the most essential factor in an organization. Unfortunately, this element has been the most neglected among all the components that make up a modern administrative system. It is strange that no academic institution in Palestine offers a major in public administration at a time when this specialization is badly needed to build good government institutions. Regarding post-service training in public management, little effort has been spent in making the idea of a central training institute a reality. Reform remains an abstract concept that needs to be translated into action. It is very important to identify the instruments of change that can produce the needed results. Undoubtedly the principal instrument of change is the political leadership, without which no significant reforms can take place. Unfortunately, certain elements in the current Palestinian leadership perceive reform as a potential threat to their political survival, and hence they are not expected to actively participate in reform efforts. In view of the weak position of both the secular opposition groups and the local intelligentsia, combined with the extremist political agenda of the Islamic fundamentalist movement, the drive for reform will continue to be problematic in the foreseeable future. Furthermore, up to this moment, no integrated strategy or model exists to direct reform programs. There are only disparate steps that respond to demands and pressures coming from different directions. No discussion is being conducted about the most appropriate strategy to be followed under the circumstances. Is the political leadership following a radical, comprehensive reform model or an incremental one? What kind of vision does the leadership have? Is there any list of priorities? These questions and many more remain to be answered.

In order to carry out its mission, and create an environment that can facilitate economic growth, the new Palestinian public administration should fulfill the following conditions:

1. Place more emphasis on the quality of public services delivery.
2. Show a strong commitment to social and economic development.
3. Demonstrate concern for social equity and justice.
4. Pledge an unequivocal commitment to transparency and accountability.

5. Maintain a healthy and cooperative relationship with the private sector.

Public-private partnership is a strong trend in today's world. It could, as well, be a good recipe for the Palestinian economy if such partnership is seriously considered and thoroughly studied. The events of the last two years, despite all the miseries and pains it inflicted on both sides of the divide, could be exploited by the political decision-makers in Palestine to start the courageous process of reform in order to create sound bases for a future and viable Palestinian state that will live in peace and harmony with its neighbors.

NOTES

Chapter 1

1. Philip Hitti, *History of Syria: Including Lebanon and Palestine*, (London: McMillan and Co., Ltd, 1951), p.664.
2. *Ibid.*
3. George G. Arnakis, *The Near East in Modern Times* Vol 1 "The Ottoman Empire and the Balkan States to 1900" (New York, Austin, Jenkins Publishing Company, 1969), p.373.
4. David Kushner, *Palestine in the Late Ottoman Empire: Political, Social and Economic Transformation* (Jerusalem: Yad Izhak Ben-Zvi Press, 1985) p.9.
5. Hardy Wickwar, *The Modernization of Administration in the Middle East* (Beirut, Khayats,1963), p.20.
6. Adolphus Slade, quoted in Bernard Lewis, *A Middle East Mosaic, Fragments of Life, Letters and History* (New York: Random House, 2000), pp 240-241.
7. Lord Kinros, *The Ottoman Centuries: The Rise and Fall of the Turkish Empire* (New York: Morrow Quill Paperbacks, 1977), p. 516
8. *Ibid.*, pp7-8
9. Carlton Hayes and Charles Woolsey Cole, *History of Europe since 1500* (New York:The MacMillan Company,1959), 461.
10. *Ibid.*, p 404
11. Kinros, *op.cit.*, p. 474
12. *Ibid.*
13. *Ibid.*, p.476.
14. Wickwar, *op.cit.*, p.46.
15. Kinros, *op.cit.*, p.476.

16. Wickwar, *op.cit.*, p.47.
17. *Ibid.*
18. *Ibid.*, p.48.
19. Kushner, *op.cit.*, p59
20. Alfred Bonne, *State and Economics in the Middle East: A Society in Transition*((London: Kegan Paul, Trench, Trubner and Co., Ltd., 1968), p.43.
21. *Ibid.*, p.45.
22. Wickwar, *op.cit.*, p.22
23. George Antonius, *The Arab Awakening: The Story of the Arab National Movement* (Beirut: Khayats, 1955) p.107
24. Hitti, *op.cit.*, p 669.
25. *Ibid.*, p 667
26. Esco Foundation For Palestine, *Palestine : A Study of Jewish Arab and British Policies*, 2 vols (New Haven : Yale University Press, 1947) p. 297
27. Namik Kamal, quoted in Lewis, *op.cit.*, p. 241.

Chapter 2

1. Norman Bentwich, *England in Palestine* (London: Kegan Paul, Trench, and Co, Ltd, 1932), p.22.
2. Bahjat Sabri, *Falastine Khilal Al-Harb Al-Alamiyat Al-ula Wama Bahdaha, 1914-1920* (Palestine during the First World War and After 1914-1920), (Jerusalem: Arab Studies Society, 1982), pp .147-148.
3. Hayes and Cole, *op.cit.*, p.484
4. *Report to the General Assembly of the United Nations Special Committee on Palestine,* Vol 2, Appendix and Maps 22,U.N. Doc. A/364 Add.1 (Sept 9, 1947).
5. Ruth Lapidoth and Moshe Hirsch (eds)," The Balfour Declaration 2 November 1917" In *The Arab- Israel Conflict and Its Resolution: Selected Documents* (The Netherlands: Martinus Nijhof Publishers, 1992) p.20.
6. Kamel Mahmoud Khelleh, *Falastine Wal-Intidab Al-Baritani, 1922-1939* (Palestine and the British Mandate, 1922- 1939) (Tripoli, Libya, 1982), p. 84.
7. Lapidoth and Hirsch, *op.cit.*, p.23.
8. *Ibid.*, p. 24.
9. Khelleh, *op.cit.*, pp 65-66.

10. Sabri, *op.cit.*, p.146.
11. Anthony Nutting, *The Arabs* (London: 1964), pp321-322.
12. Bentwich, *op.cit.*, p.54.
13. Khelleh, *op.cit.*, pp 751-752.
14. Bentwich, *op.cit.*, p. 103.
15. Khelleh, *op.cit.*, p.67.
16. *Ibid.*
17. Sabri, *op.cit.*, p.152.
18. In John Norton Moore (ed), *The Arab-Israeli Conflict* (New Jersey: Princeton University Press, 1977), pp 878-883.
19. Sabri, *op.cit.*, p.155.
20. Larry Luke and Edward keith-Roach, *The Handbook of Palestine and Trans-Jordan*
21. (London: 1934), p.312.
21. Esco Foundation For Palestine, *op.cit.*, p.304.
22. Khelleh, *op.cit.*, p.84.
23. Sabri, *op.cit.*, p.236
24. Khelleh, *op.cit.*, 85.
25. *Ibid.* p.893.
26. W. F. Bustany, *The Palestine Mandate: Invalid and Impracticable* (Beirut: The American Press, 1936), p.79.
27. Hisham Sharabi, *Nationalism and Revolution in the Arab World: The Middle East and North Africa* (New Jersey, D.U and Nestrand and Co.,Ltd, 1966), p.37.

Chapter 3

1. Hussein Abu-Alnamel, *Qita Ghaza (1948-1967), Tatawworat Iktisadiah Wassiasiah Wajtimaiah Waaskariah,*(Gaza Strip (1948-1967), Economic Political Social and Military Developments), (Beirut: Palestine Research Center, 1979), p.21.
2. Aqel Hayder Abidi, *Jordan: A Political study (1948-1957)*, (London: Asia Publishing House, 1965), p.50
3. Abu-Alnamel, *op.cit.*, pp 22-23.
4. Aref Al-Aref, Annakba: *Nakbat Beit-Al-Makdis Wal Ferdos Almafkood* (The Clamity: The Calamity of Jerusalem and the lost Paradise) (Bierut, Sidon: Modern Library Publishing House, 1964) Vol, IV, p.377.

5. Jamil Hilal, *Al-Daffa Al-Gharbiyah: Al-Tarkib Al-Ikitasadi Wal-Ijtimaie (1948-1974)* (The West Bank: The Economic and Social Structure (1948-1974) (Beirut: PLO Research Center, 1975), p.32.
6. Ann Deadran, *Jordan* (London: Robert Hale Ltd.,1958), p.77.
7. Edwin Van Deusen, *The Development of Democratic Institutions in the Hashemite Kingdom of Jordan* (Unpublished M.A Thesis, American University of Beirut, 1955), p.140.
8. Deadran, *op.cit.*, p.99
9. Jordan Official Gazette, *The Constitution* (January 8, 1952)
10. Hani Kheir (ed), *Majmuat Al-Bayanat Al-Wizariyah Al-Urduniah* (Collection of Jordanian Cabinet Statements) (Amman: Jordanian Press, Date of publication not mentioned), p.103.
11. Government of Jordan, Department of Statistics, *Statistical Yearbook* (Amman, 1966).
12. Government of Jordan, Department of Statistics, *Statistics of Classified Government Employees for 1966, Table No 1: Distribution of Classified Employees According to Muhafaza, Sex and Percentage* (Amman: Department of Statistics Press,1966).
13. *Jordan Official Gazette*, March 1, 1953.
14. *Jordan Official Gazette*, August 18, 1954.
15. *Jordan Official Gazette*, April 3, 1955.
16. Abidi, *op,cit.*, p.144.
17. Amnon cohen, *Political Parties in the West Bank Under the Jordanian Regime (1949- 1967)* (Ithaca: Cornel University Press, 1982), p.38.
18. *Ibid.*
19. Government of Jordan, Department of Statistics, *Statistical Yearbook,* (Amman:1966).
20. Khalid Al-Hassan, " *Limatha Narfod Al-Mamlakah Al-Arabia Al-Muttahida* (Why We Reject The United Arab Kingdom) (Al-Taliah, No.4, April, 1972).
21. International Bank For Reconstruction and Development, *The Economic Development of Jordan* (Baltimore: John Hopkins Press, 1957), p.5.
22. *Jordan Official Gazette*, April 16, 1952.
23. *Jordan official Gazette*, February 16, 1952.
24. *Jordan Official Gazette*, May 1, 1955.
25. *Jordan Official Gazette*, February 1, 1954.
26. *Jordan official Gazette*, January 1, 1959.

27. Hilal, *op.cit.*, p.19.
28. Peter Snow, *Hussein: a Biography* (London: Barrie and Jenkins, 1972), p. 150

Chapter 4

1. Abu-Al-namel, *op.cit.*, p.29
2. *Ibid.*
3. *Ibid.*
4. *Ibid.*, p.192
5. *Ibid.*, p.194.
6. *Ibid.*, p. 196
7. *Ibid.*, pp 222-223.
8. Hilal, *op.cit.*, p.19.
9. Abu-Al-namel, *op.cit.*, p.40.

Chapter 5

1. *Israel Official Gazette*, No. 2064, 1967, p.2690
2. Meron Benvenisti, "1986 Report, Demographic, Economic, legal, Social and Political Developments in the West Bank" *(The West Bank Data Base Project)* (Jerusalem, 1986), pp 41-42.
3. *Ibid.*
4. *Ibid.*
5. *Al-Quds Newspaper*, December 13,1991.
6. Benvenisti, *op.cit.*, p 46.
7. *Yediot Ahronot Newspaper*, Friday, January 31,1992.
8. *Ibid.*
9. Benvenisti, *op.cit.*, 37.
10. *Ibid.*, p. 38.
11. *Ibid.*, p.42.
12. *Ibid.*, pp 18-19.
13. *The Jerusalem Post Newspaper*, October 20, 1988.
14. Amira Hass " The Civil Administration was never Disbanded," *Haaretz Newspaper*, Wed, 3 July, 2002
15. Benvenisti, *op.cit.*

Chapter 6

1. Hass, *op.cit.*
2. United Nations, *UNCTAD* " The Palestinian Economy: Achievements of the Interim Period and Tasks for the Future," (Geneva, 2001), p.10.
3. Arab Thought Society, "Democratic Formation in Palestine," (Jerusalem, March, 1999), p.30.
4. *Al-Quds Newspaper*, Friday, October 17, 1997.
5. Arab Thought Society, *op.cit.*, p.37.
6. UNCTAD, *op.cit.*, p. 10.
7. *Al-Quds Newspaper*, Saturday, September 2, 2000
8. Arab Thought Society, *op.cit.*, 24.
9. Palestinian Legilative Council, *Attakrir Almuqaddam Mena Allajnah Alkhassah Almukallafat Mena-Almajlis Altashrie Howla Takrir Raes Hayat Al-rakabah Al-ammah Al-Sanawi Al-Awwal,1996.* Report of the PLC's Special Committee on the General Controllers' First Report for 1996 . (unpublished report submitted to the PLC on 28th July,1997)
10. Palestinian Legislative Council, *op .cit.*, pp 27-28.
11. Donald E. Klinger, *Public Personnel Management: Contexts and Strategies*, New Jersey: Prentice-Hall, 1980, p 291
12. UNCTAD, *op.cit.*, p.23.
13. *Jerusalem Times Newspaper*, The Complete Text of the PLC Reform Charter Presented to President Arafat, May 23, 2002.
14. UNCTAD, *op.cit* p.23.
15. Birzeit University, Developmental Studies Program, *Takrir Al-Tanmiyeh Al-Bashariah, Falastine 1998-1999,* Report on Manpower Development, Palestine 1998-1999, September 1999.
16. Council For Foreign Relations, *Strengthening Palestinian Public Institutions*, New York, 1999.
17. *Al-Quds Newspaper*, Interview with the Deputy Finance Minister in the PNA, Monday, April 26, 1999.
18. Arab Thought Society, *op.cit.*, p. 17.
19. Center for Policy Analysis on Palestine, Washington D.C, *Information Brief,* "The Palestinian Economy Post Oslo: Unsustainable Development," NO,79, July 11, 2001.
20. Quoted in Lewis, *op.cit.*, p. 219.

21. Sarah Graham-Brown, *Palestinians and Their Society* 1880-1946 (London: Quartet Books, 1980), p 21.
22. Saad El-Shazly, quoted in Lewis, *op.cit.*, p. 247
23. Graham-Brown, *op.cit.*, p.19.

Chapter 7

1. Robert D Denhardt, *Public Administration: An Action Orientation* (7th edition) (New York: Harcourt College Publishers, 1999), pp 234-237.
2. Nicholas Henry, *Public Administration and Public Affairs* (7th edition) (New Jersey: Prentice Hall, 1999), p 304.
3. Palestinian Central Bureau of Statistics, *Workforce Survey: Basic Results, Period of January-March 1999.*, Ramallah, June-July 1999, p.63
4. Arab Thought Society, *"Shuun Tanmawiyeh,"* op.cit., p.37
5. *Al-Quds Newspaper*, "A Seminar on Women participation in Local Councils< Thursday, June 20, 2000
6. Usamah Shahwan, *"Alwadh Alidari lilmaraat fe alidiara alamah alfalestiniah"* "The Administrative Status of Women in Palestinian Public Administration,"" unpublished Research (Arabic), Bethlehem University, July 2000.
7. UNDP, Program of Assistance to the Palestinian People, *"Report of the Mission to the Palestinian Territories, May 14- June 3, 1995,"* Jerusalem
8. *Al-Nahar Newspaper*, Interview with the Palestinian Public Works and Housing Minister, June 16, 2002, (internet version).
9. Al Sabil Newspaper, Interview with Muawiya Al-Masri, A Palestinian Legislative Council Member, July 3, 2002.

INDEX

A

Abdul-Aziz, Sultan, 2
Abdul-Hamid II, Sultan, 3-5, 10
Abdullah I, King, 24
Accords, see Oslo
absentee property, 58
accountability, xvii, xiv, 88, 95, 106
  lack of, 104
administrative divisions of Palestine:
  under the Ottomans, 1-2
  under the British Mandate, 13-15
  under the Jordanians, 26-28
  under Israeli military government, 45-46
Agricultural Bank, 17
agricultural cooperatives, 53
agricultural tax (tithe), 10
Al-Aqsa, xv
Al-Husseine, Haj Amin, 23
Al-Majali, Hazza, 27
All-Palestine Government, 24, 39
ANERA, 92
Arab Higher Committee, 24
Arab League, 24-25
Arab Legion, 23
annexation of East Jerusalem, 45-46
Arafat, Yasser, 63, 65-66, 68-69, 74, 97-99, 101, 104
authority, see Palestinian National Authority
autonomy, 9, 17, 25, 62
  economic, 63

B

Balfour Declaration, 16, 18, 22, 102
basic law (constitution), 67, 79, 97
British Mandate in Palestine:
  administrative policies, 19-22
  civil administration, 14-19
  High Commissioner, 17, 19-21
  judicial system, 17-19
  local councils, 19-20
  order-in-council, 16
  military courts, 18-19
  municipal corporation ordinance, 20-21, 33
budgeting, 16, 56, 65, 66, 74-75, 77; see also fiscal management in Palestine
bureaucracy, see Palestinian civil service
by-laws, 65

C

chairman, see Arafat
civil administration in Palestine

under the British Mandate, 14
under Israeli military government, 46-47, 52, 62
assessment of civil administration under occupation, 54-55
civil society, xvi, 95, 105
Clayton, General, 16
commercial courts, 6
confessional decentralization, 9
Congress of Jericho, 24
Covenant of the League of Nations, 14-15
Conseil d' etat, 6-7
co-optation, 5
Council of Justice, 5
courts, see judicial systems

D

decentralization, 76; see also confessional decentralization
defense ministry of Israel, 47
defense regulations, 37
development budget, 79
diaspora, 98
district commissioner, see British administration
distrust of authority, 82-83
duplicity, 70

E

economic protocols of paris, 63
East Jerusalem, see Jerusalem
Egyptian administration of Gaza, 39-43
constitutional order, 40
employment, see Palestinian civil service
European Union, 74

F

Fatah, 62
fatalism, 84
family, influence of, 83
First World War, 4, 7, 13
fiscal management in Palestine, 74-76
French procedural codes, 6

G

Gaza, xiv, 13, 16, 19, 41-43, 47, 51-52, 65, 74, 76-77, 89, 98-99, 102-103
Gaza-Jericho agreement, 64,
General Controller's report, 66
Grass-root movement, 53-54

H

hegemony, 77
Hague Convention, 15
High commissioner, see British administration
hospitality, 83-84
human resource management in Palestine, 72-74

I

International Bank for Reconstruction and Development, 30
Intifada (uprising), xi, xv, 54
Israel, xiii, xiv, 23, 25, 35, 45, 48, 51, 53, 104
executive review committees, 50

J

Janissary, 10
Jerusalem, 8, 13, 18, 23, 25, 25-26, 46
Jericho conference, 24-25
Jewish Agency, 49

Jewish immigration into Palestine, 49
Jewish settlements, xiv, 19, 48-50, 58
Job-classification, 71
Jordanian administration in the West Bank, 23-37
    administrative policies, 35-37
    law of village administration, 33
    municipalities ordinance of 1955, 31-33, 36, 50, 56, 76
Jordanian constitution of 1952, 30
Jordanian Chamber of deputies, 25, 28
Jordanian Senate, 25, 28
Judicial system in Palestine, 79-81
    under the Ottomans, 6-7
    under the British Mandate, 17-19
    under the Jordanians, 30-31
    under Israeli military government, see military orders
junta, 4

K

kinship, 83,
Koran, 5

L

League of Nations, 14
    Covenant of, 15
Legislations in Palestine:
    law of local councils, 76, 78
    law of the judiciary, 80-81
    law of the civil service, 67, 71, 73
    law for the constitution of civil courts, 80
    law of the Palestinian NGOs, 67
    law for the election of Palestinian local councils, 67
    law of the fiscal authority, 67
    law for the independence of the judiciary, 67
Likud government, 47
local government:
    under the British Mandate, 19-22
    under the Jordanians, 31-35
    under Israeli military government, 51-53
    under the Palestinian National Authority, 76-78
    financing of, 78-79
local universities, 90

M

Mahmud ll, Sultan, 3, 5
management:
    fiscal, 74-78
    human resources, 72-74
    natural resources
Mandate, se British Mandate
Memluks, 1
Mesopotamia, 14
military government in Palestine:
    the British, 13-14
    the Egyptian in Gaza, 39-41
    the Israeli in the West Bank, 46-49
military orders:
    of the British Mandatory authorities, 17
    of the Israeli occupation forces, 49-51, 63, 103
    impact on public administration, 49-51
millets (religious communities), 9
mukhtars (community headmen), 20, 24, 41, 52, 57
municipalities, see local govern-

N

Nabulsi, Suleiman, 29
Nasser, Abdul, 41
Near East, 1
nepotism, 27, 62, 80, 83; see also patronage
non-government organizations, 72, 92-93, 104

O

order-in-council, see British Mandatory administration
Oslo Accords, xiv, 61, 64-65, 88, 104
Ottoman administrative policies, 7-11
Ottoman constitution of 1876, 5
Ottoman laws:
   land law, 6
   law of the Wilayats, 2
   penal code, 6

P

Palestinian government:
   central bureau of statistics, 68
   civil service, 68-72, 90, 98
   civil service commission, 71, 98
   council of ministers, 67-68
   economic council for development and reconstruction, 68-70
   general control bureau, 68-69, 71
   judiciary, 79-81
   legislative council (PLC), 65, 67, 69-70, 74, 76
   monitoring committee, 69
Palestine Liberation Organization (PLO), 41, 48, 52, 56, 72, 98, 104
Palestine National Authority (PNA), xiv, xvi, 61-69, 71-76, 79-81, 89-98, 104-105
Palestinian refugees, xiv, 41-42
Palestinian economy, 59, 63
Pasha, Muhammad Ali, 2
patriarchal family, 83
patronage, 61, 75, 87; see also nepotism
political appointees, 87-89
president, see Arafat
presidential decree, 80
promotion, 73
public-private partnership, 107

Q

quasi-legislative powers, 5
quasi-monopolies, 75

R

rational model of organization, 81
reform, 94-100, 106
   charter, 74,
   plan, 95-97
Religious High Council, 5; see also Ottoman judicial system
shariat (Islamic law), 3, 6
Samuel, Herbert, 17,
settlements, see Jewish
Shazily, Saed El, 82
Shukeiry, Ahmed, 41
shura (consultation), 4
socio-cultural context, 81-82
sovereignty, 62, 91-92, 102
supreme planning council, 50
supreme court, see judiciary
Sykes-Picot Agreement, 18, 22
Syria, 1, 102

T

tanzimat (Ottoman reforms), 2-3, 5-

6, 27, 102
training, 72-73, 105-106
government institute, 73, 106
Treaty of Sevres, 14
transparency, xvi-xvii, 75
Turkish, see Ottoman

U

United Nations Development Program (UNDP), 73, 92, 94
United Nations Relief and Works Agency (UNRWA), 42
United states Agency for International Development (USAID), 37, 92
United States of America, xiii, 74, 79, 97
Supreme Court of, xvi

village councils, see local government

W

wasta (patronage), 83
West Bank, xiii-xiv, 13, 18, 23, 26, 43, 45, 49-54, 57, 61-65, 74, 76-77, 89, 97-99, 102-103
women, 89- 91

Y

Young Turks, 4, 7, 10

Z

Zionist Federation, 22, 102

village leagues, 47-48, 52

ABOUT THE AUTHOR

Usamah Shahwan is an Associate Professor of Public Administration in the Faculty of Business Administration and Accounting at Bethlehem University. He is the author of two other books: *Administrative Thought and the Crisis of Contemporary Man*, and *State Administration: Concepts and Development*, both in Arabic. He has published several articles and empirical studies on public management and entrepreneurship in professional journals in the Middle East, England and the United States.

Dr. Shahwan received his doctorate from the University of Southern California's School of Public Administration in 1984. He holds a bachelor's and a master's degree in public administration from the American University of Beirut.

Prior to joining Bethlehem University, Dr. Shahwan taught at An-Najah University in Nablus, Hebron University and Al-Quds University and for one semester at USC. He was on the editorial boards of the university research journals of An-Najah and Hebron Universities. He also served as consultant to several local and international agencies including United Nations Conference on Trade and Development (UNCTAD), United Nations Development Program (UNDP) and the International Peace Center in Jerusalem.